The Nightmare of God
The Book Of Revelation

By David Berrigan

Photo Etchings by Tom Lewis-Borbley

WIPF & STOCK · Eugene, Oregon

The Nightmare of God

Daniel Berrigan

Photo Etchings and Afterword by Tom Lewis-Borbely

Wipf and Stock Publishers
199 W 8th Ave, Suite 3
Eugene, OR 97401

The Nightmare of God
The Book of Revelation
By Berrigan, Daniel
Copyright©1983 Catholic Worker Books
ISBN 13: 978-1-60608-470-0
Publication date 4/13/2009
Previously published by Rose Hill Books, 1983

SERIES FOREWORD

Daniel Berrigan is one of the most influential American Catholics of the twentieth century. A Jesuit priest, poet, and peacemaker, he has inspired countless people of faith and conscience to pursue the gospel vision of a world without war or nuclear weapons. Born in 1921, he entered the Society of Jesus in 1939, was ordained in 1952, and in 1957 published his first book of poetry, *Time Without Number*, which won the prestigious Lamont Poetry Award.

Since then Daniel Berrigan, my friend and Jesuit brother, has published over fifty books, including the award-winning play, *The Trial of the Catonsville Nine* (1970); an autobiography, *To Dwell in Peace* (1987); and many journals, essays, poetry collections, and scripture commentaries. Dan maintained close friend friendships with Thomas Merton and Dorothy Day. He also co-founded the Catholic Peace Fellowship and Clergy and Laity Concerned about Vietnam. But because of his early peace work, church authorities banished him to Latin America in 1966 and 1967. In early 1968, he traveled to Hanoi with Howard Zinn to experience firsthand the horrors of U.S. war-making and to rescue three U.S. soldiers who had been captured.

On May 19, 1968, with his brother Philip and other friends, he burned military draft files using homemade napalm in Catonsville, Maryland—an action which galvanized millions against the Vietnam war. For this creative nonviolence, Dan was tried, convicted, and sentenced to years in prison. In April of 1970, however, he went underground, eluding the FBI, and continued to draw widespread attention to his antiwar message. He was finally arrested in August, and imprisoned in Danbury, Connecticut until February 1972.

He continued to write and speak against war and nuclear weapons throughout the 70s. On September 9, 1980, both he and Philip participated in the first Plowshares Action, a protest at the General Electric Plant at King of Prussia, Pennsylvania. He faced ten years in prison, but was eventually sentenced to time served.

Since the early 1970s, Dan has lived in New York City with his Jesuit community. He continues to give lectures, conduct retreats, publish books of poetry and scripture study—and get arrested for his protests against war, injustice, and nuclear weapons. He remains a clear voice of resistance to war, gospel nonviolence, and peace for humanity.

Throughout his faithful, peacemaking life, Daniel Berrigan has consistently said no to every war, injustice, and weapon of violence. And with every no he accepts the cost. And he does not give up. Nominated many times for the Nobel Peace Prize, Dan often finds himself with friends before some judge and sitting on ice in some dismal holding cell. Such is the mark of a prophet, the sign of an apostle of peace.

"We have assumed the name of peacemakers," Dan writes in *No Bars to Manhood*,

> but we have been, by and large, unwilling to pay any significant price. And because we want the peace with half a heart and half a life and will, the war, of course, continues, because the waging of war, by its nature, is total—but the waging of peace, by our own cowardice, is partial. There is no peace because there are no peacemakers. There are no makers of peace because the making of peace is at least as costly as the making of war, at least as exigent, at least as disruptive, at least as liable to bring disgrace and prison and death in its wake.

Foreword

"The only message I have to the world is: we are not allowed to kill innocent people," he told the court during his Plowshares Eight trial.

> We are not allowed to be complicit in murder. We are not allowed to be silent while preparations for mass murder proceed in our name, with our money, secretly. . . . It's terrible for me to live in a time where I have nothing to say to human beings except, 'Stop killing.' There are other beautiful things that I would love to be saying to people. There are other projects I could be very helpful at. And I can't do them. I cannot. Because everything is endangered. Everything is up for grabs. Ours is a kind of primitive situation, even though we would call ourselves sophisticated. Our plight is very primitive from a Christian point of view. We are back where we started. 'Thou shalt not kill'; we are not allowed to kill. Everything today comes down to that—everything.

I am very grateful to Wipf and Stock Publishers for republishing some of Dan's classic works in a series, books which influenced millions of people when they first appeared. I hope these books will be studied, passed around to friends and neighbors, and promoted far and wide. They still offer great hope, wisdom, and encouragement.

In the life and words of Daniel Berrigan we discover new faith in the God of peace and courage to pursue God's reign of peace. We see signs and guideposts for the path ahead, toward a new future of peace. And we find strength to take our own stand for justice and disarmament, to take another step forward on the road to peace and nonviolence. May these books inspire us to become, like Daniel Berrigan, peacemakers in a world of war.

—John Dear
Cerrillos, New Mexico
August 2007

*To my sisters and brothers
of the Plowshares 8:*

> ***Molly***
> ***Anne***
> ***John***
> ***Elmer***
> ***Carl***
> ***Dean***
> ***Philip***

Contents

1	Introduction: The Day We Dug a Grave and Walked On
9	Cracking the Code: A Glossary of Images
19	The Nightmare of God: And How He Awakened
33	The Book No One Could Open
47	The Day After Doomsday
59	Idols: i.e., Whatever Turns You On
67	The Beast from the Sea
85	Seven Bowls of Wrath: Come Let Us Eat and Drink, for Tomorrow We Die
95	The Day the Empire Fell, and How, and Why
109	The Feast of Carrion
117	Afterword

Introduction: The Day We Dug A Grave, and Walked On

(January, 1976: District of Columbia Jail)

I'm sitting here looking through the usual bolts and bars and remote filthy windows. Into what? After a while both your eyes seem cataracted, the distance is a filmy veil. But that isn't your eyes' fault; it's just that the vast useless windows aren't meant to be seen through at all; a use that escaped the builders, who were interested only in creating a world out of this world, into which were plunged those who had proven themselves unfit for this world.

We're in jail again, Phil and I, together on the same old trip that landed us in trouble in the sixties. Then we burned papers, now we dig graves. The latter seems to offer a "better future," in view of the nuclear plan to ration out life and multiply the dead.

People like us, who learned our trade in Hamlet and the Book of Ecclesiasticus, have a double consolation to bear us up on bad days. We're in touch with a long tradition, and given Herman Kahn and the Pentagon, we'll never be out of work until we so to speak, tumble over dead into our own handiwork.

Here's a little poem about our crime:

Zen Shovel
we dug a grave
on the white house lawn
The fuzz were furious
dragged us away

But the little shovel
an industrious angel
went on digging
to judgment day

Down down it dug
and down and down
Up up it piled

that bloody spoils

And the angel whispered
to my puzzled soul
*The further you dig
into origins
the deeper deeper
origins get.*

Well, the continuity is intriguing, not to say vivifying. Jesus never dug a grave, for Himself or anyone else, as far as we know. But He did occupy one — briefly. Maybe we, digging graves at the White House and the Pentagon, are getting necrophilic, though I don't think so. We reflected together this morning on the first chapter of Revelation, where He says: I have died but I am living.... I have authority over death and the land of the dead.... At least He's biophilic, that's consoling and More! if He's in charge of the dead, may He lead us out — on our feet!

One of the difficult things is that no one, or almost no one, sees the mortal danger we're in. In a strange backhanded way, one feels like bowing in the direction of Herman Kahn. He truly thinks the unthinkable; not to stress discourteously the fact that he helps create it too. Trouble is, most people won't even think the thinkable; which is to say, "You don't really all have to die; there's nothing in the world, including our own infested brains, our hopelessness, our prodigal self-love, that says — things have to end up on the ash heap, bones, people, tin cans, a rubble. Bad as we are, we don't have to be that bad!"

It isn't so much that we have The Bomb, as that The Bomb has us. Fascinated, fixated on death. You see it in people's eyes, a deadening plague, a tragedy, unresolved, sitting there like a cry. How is it I see in their eyes something I don't see in my own? As though their retina held an image, self-created, that mine wouldn't admit to?

Well I see tragedy too; but of a different kind indeed.

Revelation says: Come, Lord Jesus. The nuclear arsonists say: Let it all come down. We've got an enemy.

Meantime the enemy says: Let it all come down. We've got an enemy who's got an enemy.

Let me hasten to add: I don't think Jesus doesn't think everything's coming down. Indeed, indeed. In Chapter 13, the whole right tight order of things flips over on its head; the new disorder culminates in a kind of last ditch moral nightmare. People begin worshipping a mysterious slouching beast, following after, bowing down, offering gifts, making much of zero; and worse. Love of death, idolatry, fear of life; that roughshod trek of war and warmakers through the world, hand in hand with death. Long live death!

They wouldn't worship if they weren't in love. Or if they weren't in fear. The second being a state as devouring, at least, as the first. I think the clue is the second, masquerading as the first. Just as the beast is the ape of God; to do some things successfully, you have above all to hide what you're up to. In this way fear can ape love, death can demand a tribute owed to life, the ape can play God.

Such reflections are of course ill received by some: those to whom the state is a given, the Church a given, Western culture a given, war a given; likewise consumerism, taxpaying. All the neat slots of existence into which one is to fit, birth to death and every point between. Nothing to be created, no one to be responsible to, nothing to risk, no objections to lodge.... Life is a mechanical horizontal sidewalk, of the kind you sometimes ride at airports between buildings. One is carried along, a zonked spectator.

Well. Revelation says John says he saw Jesus. The claim of so many freaks and crazies across the world, across the centuries. I asked a class of students once, merely to get some hunches started, to translate this: "I saw one standing, a sword issuing from his mouth, a light around his body." John, who was no weakling, said he fell down like a stone at the sight. How do you translate what he saw? Or what Revelation said he saw?

The students had no ideas on the subject.

But suppose John made a breakthrough?

He deserved one, being all but broken. In a slave camp, in exile on a rock. Because, as he said, he preached God's word, the truth Jesus revealed. What kind of preaching brings that kind of punishment? So the question gets pushed back.

The Spirit took hold of me, on the Lord's day.

What kind of life gets seized by the Spirit?

The hellish fact is that many people lose hope.

Anyway, here's my translation of that breakthrough. It's the gratitude that wells up in me, unforeseen, almost ecstatic, at being in jail. Now help me figure that one out! It's being here (even here) with Phil. I remember something Sam Melville wrote about Attica. Prison can be ecstasy. It's one's act of faith in choosing to be here — verified in the eyes, speech, conduct, style of another. Being here with Phil.

This hole. They say even in DC Jail, you can't go lower than we've gone. We're in deadlock: 24-hour lockup, two in a cell hardly large enough for one, sharing space with mice, rats, flies and assorted uninvited fauna. Food shoved in the door, filth, degradation.

And I wouldn't choose to be anywhere else on the planet. I think we've landed on turf where the breakthrough occurs. I think it's occurred already.

The noise tonight is enough to drive one's mind up the wall like a scared roach. I wonder if hell is a place where noise is the only punishment? Last night there were three fires on the upper tiers, a dangerous thing when a hundred men are locked up tight. Now, in addition to the four TVs going full blast, there's the rhythmic beating on the bars and walls — cause unknown.

We had a short exchange with the Lieutenant this PM. He came by stony-faced, Phil asked if he had a moment.

"Any possibility of other housing here, Lieutenant?"
He'd see to it. Passed on. On his way back, he paused at our cell door.

"Don't want to start a big discussion, but why don't you men get out of here? You don't belong here...."

"Well, we don't feature paying money to the government." (We could be sprung by paying a hundred dollar fine.)

"I know all that, but what about your health? This is a pretty rough place...." He peered into our hutch like a keeper of rabbits.

"We get enough to eat and we manage to exercise —"

"In here?" He looked at our considerable frames in that inconsiderable space.

"Sure. We do pushups and yoga."

"OK. Well, I'll see about a housing change...." He stalked off. It was a touch of humanity in a dark place.

So we go on studying Revelation. We're rendered thoughtful, amid the nightmare thicket of TV, the pounding of fists on steel, the hate and fury, by the words of John the Majestic.

We see ourselves here as a remnant of sorts, rendered modest by the times. (I like that word "rendered"; it means boiling the fat, off the soul.) Made modest also by our sins, by our drawing back, our childhood in the culture, followed by a cultural childhood. Then, John on Patmos!

Was he a kook, a vaporized freak, a *non sequitur* in a chain of logic, a broken link? We ask the question because it seemed as though the early church was facing the same question, at least by implication. And answer —

No, he suffered for Jesus and thereupon, in a link with all who suffer for the faith, he was granted this visionary sequence. Thus a logic of suffering vision held firm, hand to hand.

Or in anther image: John stands deservedly, as in a great window at Chartres, on the shoulders of Isaiah; he is upborne by the older prophet, who thus enables him to see further. To see, insofar as it is given to human eyes, "that which our hands have touched ... of the word of life." (I Jn. 1:1)

The seven churches evidently also deserved the vision of John, welcomed it, and believed. Thus the vision is for the community, not for John alone.

So John wrote letters to the seven churches.

We wondered how such letters would be received today. We wondered also what authority, what credentials would verify them — would it be suffering and faith, on which the apostolic authority was founded?

As to the community — it seems as though parallel rhythms were at work. Suffering faith and vision. The community worships and stands there in the world, more precisely in the imperial state. So it comes to vision. The heavens open, Jesus speaks; always through John, but to the churches.

It seems to us that when the church is faithful, the people gain enough energy to go on. I think this means something quite simple: to be and continue to be, the church. To know who we are, and to speak that word, in season and out, a word of liberation, free of the vagaries and mindlessness that cling to "movements" like predators to the running bodies of panicked deer — and bring them down.

I think that word, on the modern scene, is one of liberation from death. We are learning something of the price of that word, in repeated trials and jailings. As the crunch is on the living, the crunch tightens on the defenders of the living; the most vulnerable thing in all the world being the lives of the innocent. (Today a bishop came in from Virginia, to take part in a pro-life demo in DC. He came over here to visit us, evidently understanding that abortion and nuclear weaponry are two sides of the same hot coin, minted in hell. Not a bad insight.)

Apart from such one-night-stands of conscience, how is one to understand the sublime announcement of Christ, so often repeated: "I live for ever and ever. I was dead and now I live"? Is He no more than the shadowy master of a neutral kingdom, where life has no edge and death calls the body count? Impossible.

We thought, if He were to pass along the catwalk and pause at our cell bars, He would praise, reprove and promise; as He repeated time and again, His praise, reproof and promise to the seven churches.

Praise for our attempt at fidelity, our passion for life. Reproof: indeed he would be stern, as the letters to the churches are stern. Failure of love, broken promises, paganism in practice, cruelty of heart, cupidity, falling away from the call to excellence. We know the sinful litany — not nearly as well as He, but at least well enough to verify the word, to be put to the blush.

And the promise. "Do not fear. I am with you...." I hardly have words to say how I believe this, deeply, with all my heart. Said to Phil yesterday, "Can you imagine yourself, conjure yourself up, apart from this promise?" I said I could not; so did he. It was almost like a game: Watch me while I vaporize, then describe me, the someone who was, the nothing that is.

The promise looms large in Revelation: "Don't fear, I will come soon"; and then the ecstatic cry of the people: "Come, Lord Jesus."

Meantime. The only time we have. Meantime, you act in the world as though He had spoken the truth. That's called the ethic of the promise. So live as though He were near, near in time, near in place, the witness of our motives, our speech. As indeed He is.

That nearness of His! The millenarians love to put a stopwatch to His running, but running is not necessarily coming close; nor can a mystery be so timed. I suppose until the end of time the debate will go on among the experts: Were the early Christians millenarians of this kind, duped into an ecstatic cloud of unknowing? If so, it becomes difficult to explain their hardihood, political imagination, patience, wisdom. And then the martyrdoms.

Suppose on the other hand they were intensely aware of a spiritual presence, a Lord who was always "near," in the quite simple sense that He was not "afar," disinterested, Olympian. How indeed could He be other than near, having (and so recently) been God-with-us, human, a son of the tribe?

To the question of His coming, soon, now, tomorrow, at the end of eons, they might pose a question of their own: If He is not near, where is He?

A pressure gathered strength; to do, to suffer, to endure, to win through — a breakthrough: Himself. This is the work of the believers and of the believing church, insofar as both are to undergo a change of heart that will place me (and all) near, now and here, to Him.

In a place like the DC Jail where I scrawl these notes, perched on a top tier bunk under a limp bulb, such things come home to one with a new and poignant force. Around us, such suffering and waste, hidden away so gratuitously, with such lethal skill. The great society, hobbling along, wasted, aging, fretful, inconstant, violent, puts its best brains and resources into war and war preparation, would make of the world first its lackey, then its waste heap. It must have its domestic dumps as well; the jails where the useless and deviant are consigned. Entirely fitting too that one of the worst lime pits in the nation squats in the proud shadow of the capitol dome.

The visiting room here is an eerie five-storied echo chamber, "the rotunda." Once, a hundred years ago, it was undoubtedly a central foyer, the nerve center of the diseased project. Now it is shored up with planking, sheets of plywood. The ribbing is splayed and cracked. Under the dome day after day, misery meets misery as the families of prisoners wait listlessly (black faces invariably) for the denimed figures who issue like blue ghosts from the inner darkness. "VISIT IN THE ROTUNDA!" It has a grand sound, grandeur in a madhouse; an engraved invitation issued to pick up a welfare dole. One half hour with a family: face to face, if you're lucky. Otherwise prisoners are herded into cages along the walls, where they stare like captive fish through glass, at the transfixed faces of their visitors. In this case, you speak over a phone, forbidden touch or contact.

Touch, contact, embrace without ending. "I have come ... to liberate the captives." (Lk. 4:18-19) Come, Lord Jesus.

Cracking the Code:
A Glossary of Images

Abyss

By no means the "pure void" of Zen, a plenary nothingness of the spirit, an alert waiting on mystery. Nor the "nada" of John of the Cross, a sense of creatureliness, an almost unbearable self-awareness in view of the majesty of God. Nor the preexistent void which awaits creation; the "day before the first day."

None of these. But an infested cosmos, the demonic consciousness verified in cultural and political events and realities. A teeming welter of devils, devilish desires and appetites, the interpenetrating, loud-mouthed, cursing, despair-ridden "circles of hell."

Now and again, God allows the demons release; then they become present to the world, to us, to our structures, in a way that is more terrifying than absence or loneliness. For the creatures of the abyss are akin to all that is worst in us: our false worship, our violence, our blindness, our illusions of power and property. The demons stream out, in this vivid imagery which is a rendering of history's meaning: to take the reins of history. Or from the upper air of the world, they rain ruin down, a kind of invincible air force of hell.

Open the human heart: an abyss. Open the pentagon: an abyss. We are lost, except we "choose to be chosen." Then the abyss closes, its sycophants and lackeys, the servants of evil, vanish in thin air.

The world and its ploys and deceits, is the anteroom of the abyss. The sacraments exorcise it, keep its malign influence at distance. Power, as commonly desired, seized, wrestled for, practiced, is its calling card. Come in, come in!

The imperial nation is its blueprint, master plan. A kind of grandiose architectural stereotype. Pharaohs, Shahs, Colonels, city Bosses, Caudillos, all are great builders. They build their own tombs. Murder is its credit card. The credit is purportedly unlimited. Not so in fact: There is an accounting, the Book reminds.

Finally, the open heart of God is its opposite number, the opposite of the abyss being the very heart and wellspring of love: fecund, alert, providential.

From the abyss, finally, definitively, stalks the Beast. The Book says with a kind of courageous and sublime calm: "He will go off to be destroyed." (Rev. 17:8) Need one add, to destroy himself?

Angels

They are everywhere in the Book of Revelation. Their roles are both delight and terror; they are spirits of worship, messengers, interpreters, oath swearers, harvesters of first fruits and of wrath. At times they seem like very emanations of God, His breath or voice; at others they cling to earth, animistic, immanent, the "other side" of trees, grass, sea, land. They stand at distance from creation, they speak from within, as we say, the soul of things.

Are there angels in jail even? It would seem so. Peter was led out of durance vile by one of these wondrous liberators. (NB One who doesn't await an angel, shouldn't go to jail.)

Then the question arises: What is one to make of a religion that loses all sense of spirit? We seem to have landed chock-a-block in such a mad time. I was reading in jail that Billy Graham, quite recovered from recent Blight House embarrassments, assures us that Jesus, at times, may well have backslid and tipped a wine glass. Other theologians are exercised with similar crucial preoccupations.

In The Day of The Bomb, such grotesqueries would make the angels weep. Ours is a world of material slavery, spiritless, pure blah....

Quite possibly, a sense of these sublime and gentle world shakers, the angels, is the other side of the sense of our own soul. Seeing them with a third eye is another way of seeing ourselves, all we may become.

Not seeing them? What this entails, I think, is not so much a loss of a sense of identity or consciousness (those twin fetishes of self-love); say rather, a loss of conscience, of right order, of the rigor and discipline of love.

The angels guard these gates. Knowing themselves, they know God. What a community they must be!...

Wielding the BOMB, we sin against the angels too. And implacable threshing and harrowing of the material cosmos, reducing it to a chaos which is, after all, the sky-writing of our state of soul.

In Revelation, the angels stand on the earth and see, they stand by the majestic Throne. They are ministers of ceremony, singers of hymns.

Perhaps strangest of all, an angel comes bearing the "seal of the living God." (Rev. 7:2) The sign and symbol of those who love, and therefore shall live.

So the angels are servants of true knowledge, guardians of our origin and destiny. An innermost voice which reaches to the outermost. They "see God"; and they touch the tongues and minds of humans, with right choice, the savor of truth, a speech which is sane.

Whom do they seal? Can it be ourselves? Not others? And if so, by what virtue in us? Are we then set apart for special treatment in the world? This is a bloody and moot point; let us quickly add, Christians have bloodied it, rendered it moot.

Let us say (and say it in shame, and tentatively) shaking off the filthy aftermath of colonialism, slavery, third world annexations, the BOMB — let us say, we are set aside for the "special treatment" of service, love, truth.

The rest is not religion at all. It is the devil's brand and slavery.

Dragon (Also Serpent, Devil, Satan, the Accuser)
Could we add with a twist of irony — the prosecutor? In any case, he would press a case, even against Jesus. "The prince of this world approaches; he has no rights over me." (Jn. 14:30)

Even in heaven, he urges his case against the just. The government case. Against him — the Advocate, the Spirit of truth. And finally, his case is cast out, along with himself.

The point also is — he is cast in. Into the world. There, his prosecution proceeds, the evidence is collected, his polemic is razor sharp. A strange metaphor for a cruel business! In the court of secret thought as well as the petrified citadels of violence, his dossier is full. His teeth gleam, he smiles, he has all but won his case.

The "all but" is the point. Especially it is the point for those who never cared whether they won or not; a detachment which is the condition of any outcome worth talking about or striving for. The opposite of such a view is not attractive: a welter of winners and losers. The opposite to *that* is a conception of life as a gift. This latter is commended to us — by Christ, by life itself.

Such a view makes up every court on earth including the supreme one, the court of "last resort," no more than a dusty holding tank, the anteroom to the real action. It also reduces every forensic decision of this world to the status of a question mark. Is one condemned to the noose, to torture, to life — to thirty days? One takes things with the ashen equanimity that knows at least — this world can do no worse. And another court, sooner or later, will lay on you another judgment; a crown of glory.

Reward or vindication or honor — all are equally ambiguous. Who indeed is innocent, while the world goes on, and the judgment of God awaits, a shadow upon every sham sun?

And every judge in this world must hear his skeleton shake under his robes, as the gavel comes down. Is he outside the pale of judgment, in his exalted office? Or does he lie under a heavier burden than his clients, victims?

He lets the guilty, often as not, go free and easy; he commits the innocent to bondage; he paints in large alternate black and white, the murky mixed hues of conscience and act. Does not the judge look sternly upon the poor, feel the law's hold tighten in his guts as he looks down (he can only look down) on disheveled, distempered people? Does he not create a phalanx of malcontents and wards of misfortune; does he not deny the light of day to the confused and weak; does he not take bribes from skin brothers and class sisters (at least in the sense that they win from him a disposition to mercy); has he not put on the hangman's cap for the violent and mad, and summoned spontaneous mercy for the tears of crocodiles?

Let judges take warning, these guardians of real estate and unreal money. There is One who judges, whose name is neither Serpent nor Satan, whose scrutiny pierces the appearances of things, even to the joining place of body and spirit.

Eagle

He cries woe upon the world, before the event. Some call him a symbol of John, that soaring indomitable spirit.

He is also, if the expression can be pardoned, symbol of the United States Air Force. Indeed, symbol of the nation. As such, he flies high and mighty, wide and handsome over this world. Purely as symbol, he is ravenous, carnivorous, rockets in claw and a preternatural skill at smelling out living creatures, falling on them with his clutch of thunderbolts. Need one add, he is also an endangered species, besides endangering our species?

All this is of course beside the point of a learned exegesis. To most scholars of the Bible, the crimes of the US Air Force are forever beside the point. Thus does crime multiply and scholarship rot.

Kings

They fare badly in our book. Portrayed as part of a noxious web of authority; they are marked by hypocrisy, lust and violence. "They all have the same purpose, they give their power over to the beast." (Rev. 17:13) The book of Revelation ought to be burned, it is positively subversive! It will pay neither lip service, knee service, tax service, war service to the powers of this world. More, it links the fate of kings, not to God (an impeccable supposition constantly dusted off by church and state) but, horrors! — to the Beast.

Revelation is certainly not a discourse *De Potestate Regali*. It is more like a series of lightning flashes laid against thrones, victims, voids, sanctuaries, terrified faces, antics and lunacies, sanities in fool's costume, protean plans and Promethean pretensions, the tic-toc phiz of times speeded up and stopped, hustlers, fat-fingered merchants, butchers and sheriffs — yes and thank you, jails.

In the book, kings are in trouble. So are ambassadors and generals and juntas and guttural secretaries of state; also their belly dancers and silken sycophants. All the swollen-eyed hucksters and dealers in human misery! In trouble, that is, because fingered. Because unmasked, because the connections are out, gone public (as are the contracts).

The word is out. If only we knew our scripture! If we were versed in something more than the papery images of power that, day after day, make billboards of our eyes! If we knew our testament by heart, if we heard its thunder sounding in our ears, rinsing them of the foul sounds and siren enticements of this world. If we knew by heart a syllable of a word of a sentence of the sermon on the mount — why then! If we but once absorbed, welcomed, gave admittance to the voice of the eagle of Patmos — why then! Years ago, generations ago, the first Christians who dared his/her knee to a human throne would have straightened up with a snap of a switchblade; to kneel no more, to pay no more, to connive no more, to faint no more, to fond no more, to dissolve no more, to enlist no more.

And today, if one or two ancestors had only joined hands with the iron brass of John, whose other hand grasps the hand of Jesus — today we would have —

that all but unimaginable, totally coherent bread and butter ecological reality; I mean to say simply, a Christian community in America. Quite as a matter of course, a matter of the course of the sun from dawn to twilight, a matter of summer following spring, a matter of right order, of the genealogy of Jesus down, down, down, to our own city, our family. Yes, to this jail, to every jail.

Instead of this, we have — what we have: which is to say, ourselves. One hesitates to go into this matter, jail offers enough time, so to speak, to take up such subjects in private. Where perhaps right now, they belong.

To return to the kings. (We never left them.)

The kings, according to Revelation, commit fornication, they commit war; which is to say, they condemn others to die, never themselves. Then finally, when the empire is down, they commit hypocrisy. They stand far off, like a circle of sated crocodiles, shed copious tears over the ruin they have brought to pass.

Fornication is their marriage to the powers, methods, conspiracies, lunacies of this world.

Wars — consult your daily paper.

Hypocrisy — this is a rare sin of which only venturesome, publicly responsible characters, are capable. In commission of it they are aided and abetted by press agents, makeup men, and professional onion squeezers. In pursuit of this sin, Truman might pilgrimage to Hiroshima, Nixon to Hanoi, Hitler to Dachau — to weep, of course. The dead have been spared that sight.

But not this sight. The King of glory wept over Jerusalem.

Patmos

An exile work camp, where the author of Revelation (hereafter referred to for convenience sake, simply as JOHN) paid his debt to society; in consequence of his crime: namely, his faith.

And in the process, as we learn, he saw Jesus and Satan and all manner of unlikely and unearthly creatures, abysses, angels, etc. Thereby the said JOHN launched, by implication, an unlikely idea on the air of time; that prisons, these images of official and public malice and dread and moral stalemate, may become something else; a natural seed bed of visionaries. Outrageous! My own inconsiderable experience, from this end of the life span, leads me to sober approval of JOHN's intimation. I do believe that these improbable places, which a visitor to the planet would eye with a blink of disbelief, may cast up now and again, the most sublime essences, forms, symbols, revelations. Some people even grow literate here.

Patmos is quite an institution. Something like a double millstone, the pressures of human brutality and divine abandonment pressing out those furious juices....

Thank you JOHN
for saying it; for being a prisoner. Indeed we need not be vegetables or victims
our ragged lives perpetually at half mast

our wills shredded by idleness, disaffection, anomie,
eyeballs reeking with the junk tube.
There must be another way
there must be a better way
out, in, through these vicious
caravanseries, from nowhere to night,
whose bedding stinks of the hopeless sweat of have-not souls
whose air is heavy with the smoke signals of the damned.
Stand like a frozen sentry
to the here and now!...
The warden's phiz
like uncle sam's, is a perpetual spurious
lawnorder mask. He stands at attention
at the bolts and bars, barred like a macho flag.
The 50 stars
hide their faces, weep like the raped
colonies of the moon.
Ecstatics, cogs; the choices here
are not large.
Still, one learns of God
by becoming underdog.
Underdog is God (backward) gone under.
He went under.
Indeed, under ground.
SEPULTUS EST, in the old text.
Buried. The state plowed him under
Finished, dossier closed.

Prophet

    We dwell much, in our jailhouse discussion, on the meaning of this. Phil and I often feel tarred with the name "prophet." Conferred doubtlessly in good faith, but leaving us, nonetheless, queasy: a sense of being put aside or put up or put down, or all of these. But hardly put within, where we belong.

    We think the gift of prophecy is laid on every Christian tongue; a work of silence and plain speech, an unwelcome tradition brought to bear, the fruit of long loneliness, a sense of others, Eucharist, scripture, love of truth. The hope these things engender, the ability to remind the mindless, to heed the heedless, to remember the disremembered. Especially since we break the bread together, and thereupon, connect. "I tell you the truth ... this is the work of God, to believe in the One whom he has sent." (Jn. 6:29)

    We sit in this cage, where the noise scrambles all but the hardiest of heads. The guards glower at us like Hydras, the sky gapes down. We are voyagers in a ship cast adrift; locked in the vehicle of the American misadventure, a ship of fools. Sentenced to no scripture, no tradition, no landmarks, no family or friends. Yet we have all these, in abundance. A prisoner ambles by, his tortured eyes speak of a lost soul within; drugged, drugged. Another one scrubs away at the concrete floor and bars and walls, a very demon of culture, a soldier in the "war on dirt." Enlisted members of the ship's crew. Pure cutoffs. Yet they love us, because we love them, are gentle with them, share smokes and coffee and pens and cups, whatever. Prophecy? Hang on. A space voyage; walls, ceiling, thin air. Hang on.

Second Death
As if one were not enough?
The "first death" is the substance of the book. The Book of the Dead. All are bound in the same direction. Not, it must be added, by some arbitrary passage of time, creeping wrinkles, onset of disease, feeble limbs. No; death is the heart of life; the deepest urge, the savory illusion, the delicious new dawn, the rainbow with its cache of gold. It sums up every full-blown or nascent appetite, chimeric urge, grimace and derision, explosive irony of genius.

The Book of Revelation is literally placed on the world's tomb, a funerary wreath, a scripture turned to stone.

Do our wars come from nowhere, are they chancy as a storm at sea? Are human tears worthless, self-given as rain? No, we weep *because*; we war *because*. We are in love with death, we dread and fear it as the mirror image of our very souls.

I set these words down in the house of the dead.

Prisons are not merely rehearsal rooms, before a first night, a main act. They are that act, that stage. They are also mortuaries, display cases, wax museums, places where keepers and kept act out the spiritual charade of death. None but the dead need apply. Guards, social workers, medicos, shrinks, experts hustling their wares, demented planners, hangmen. And then the grid of injustice and malice outspread, into the streets, courts, classy suburbs, bankrupt academics rubbing noses with politicos and moguls — the upper echelon of the maintenance crew of hell. A wink, a pressing of flesh, judge meets executive meets monsignor meets mayor. It is all one, a subterranean intelligence lights this manse and that, this climber and that winner, a helping hand, a stroke, a nod. We understand one another, why spell it out?

All this death, this network of power and dread, of justice diminished, delayed, bargained away. Then the honorable death, the posthumous honors, the honored bomb. IT is, every bit of it, a preliminary, John declares.

He invokes a second death. Karma. The BOMB is not the last word, only the second last. IT just misses winning the show, stealing the show, owning the world. Near or not, the miss is a clean one, a final one. Even if the BOMB opens ITs maw, shouts the loudest bestial howl, bellow, whine blasphemy, ever heard this side of Armageddon. Even if, in chilling or burning fact, IT is Armageddon itself. Still penultimate. Under judgment. As also ITs dreamers, architects, keepers, owners, buyers and sellers. And those who slip ITs leash.

Though IT speak loud, IT cannot speak last. IT may condemn every living creature to death. But IT shall be condemned to the second death. IT will perish in the lake of fire IT has created.

Sun

That lovely whirling dervish, giver of life, takes a terrific beating in Revelation. It is mauled in high heaven; like ourselves, it has no place to hide. It is even at times extinguished.

More happily, the sun also serves as a jewel of glory.

And ominous. It's function is sometimes hair-raisingly like that of the BOMB. The source of all life on earth is also life's darkness, implosion.

Symbol also of the mind's light celebrated by Plato. And by Jesus, the soul on its way; "light of the world." (Jn. 8:12)

The Woman and the Whore

The two express the energies of true and false life.

The woman brings forth a son who is the ancestor of the saints. The whore is something else: She is the mistress of this world; the world of intrigue, covetousness, violence and exploitation. The woman mothers the earth and fosters its life, creating a future for all beings. She is unitive, fruitful, peaceable and wise.

The whore is finally a cannibal. She savages the world with armies, fleets, entrepreneurs. She mothers only disaster; a sleeping volcano, a furious mother of death.

Where do we come from? We come from where we are, we are where we are going. There is nothing we can claim of the mother of heaven; except that she loves us and would bring us to birth. Her word is the first word of all, creative, it is the love that breathes life.

Do we come from her? Only if we share the fate of her first born, endangered at birth by the carnivore appetites of this world. "Share the fate of..."; I mean something of simpatico, dovetailing, a like direction.

The whore? She is the ineffable creation of whorish urges: money, ego, sexual fury. The 42nd Street ethic; but also the Wall Street ethic. The low ethic of high places, where the powerful dispense something chillingly referred to as "final solutions" for the powerless.

Wrath of God

From another point of view; our own folly, and its consequence. Revelation argues that the link between personal sin and worldly misfortune is never arbitrarily forged, descending as though "from above." Nor the link between social sin and the ruin of the earth; as our own generation is witnessing.

JOHN places the drama of the seven bowls of God's wrath in high heaven. It needs also to be said, to the celestial drama there corresponds a weighty and worldly one. The bowls are concocted and poured out by our own hands.

This is not of course to declare that the innocent do not suffer, or that all suffering issues from sin. Either assertion would deny personal experience, as well as the life and death of Christ. But let us follow John's reasoning. How could God not be angry? The question wells up in the heart of any sentient being: How could God not be outraged when even we of gelid hearts are angry at the spectacle of the spoiled earth, lifelong?

There occur to me, in jail, signs of the wrath of God. First of all, the BOMB. The great and indubitable, even monstrous sign. A sign so whelming, so awesome, overmastering, claimant, self-justifying; IT is like a Stonehenge in the mind; IT is there, IT was always there, IT is part of our subconscious, rite of passage, proof of ancestry, master of the ceremony of life and death. IT gets things done, IT makes ITs point: in that measure, IT is immeasurably superior to the old gods, who were in the main, useless, silent, let us down, let us go under. Now worshipping this One And Only God, we become like IT — Number One.

The true God has turned His back on us, since we turned our backs on Him. A legion of wrath, an overt denial of grace, which is the web and tegument of the living earth, the bond of spirit and mind, and of ourselves in communion one with another. "Turn to us that we may turn to you."

Another sign: the prisoner in the end cage, but a boy. He huddles in his dirty blanket twenty hours a day, blotting out the sun, blotting us out, drugged to his ears. In his rare appearances awake, his eyes are fixed, his legs wooden. He has given up on this world, and he has no other. His sleep is death, his waking a fixated horror.

And the church; sign of His wrath. I mean a speechless, anonymous people, with their self-interest and investments intact, their property and consequence. I mean those Christians who are unrecognizable, obedient, sheepish, amid the vast numbers of lockstepping, taxpaying, consuming citizens.

And finally ourselves. In this jail, at this hour. For we are tardy and clumsy and we speak His saving word badly, and live it grudgingly. We are not wholly here. We look at the sunlight with eyes unchastened by Your hand. Do we know You, do we love You, do we bear witness to You, to the ravaged earth, to the outraged poor?

We do not; no use parrying the question.

It is not the state that has bound us hand and foot and cast us into exterior darkness. It is our own will that enslaves; we are children of wrath, whose predicament the state rushes in to conclude, enthusiast, dramatist.

Turn to us that we may turn to You.

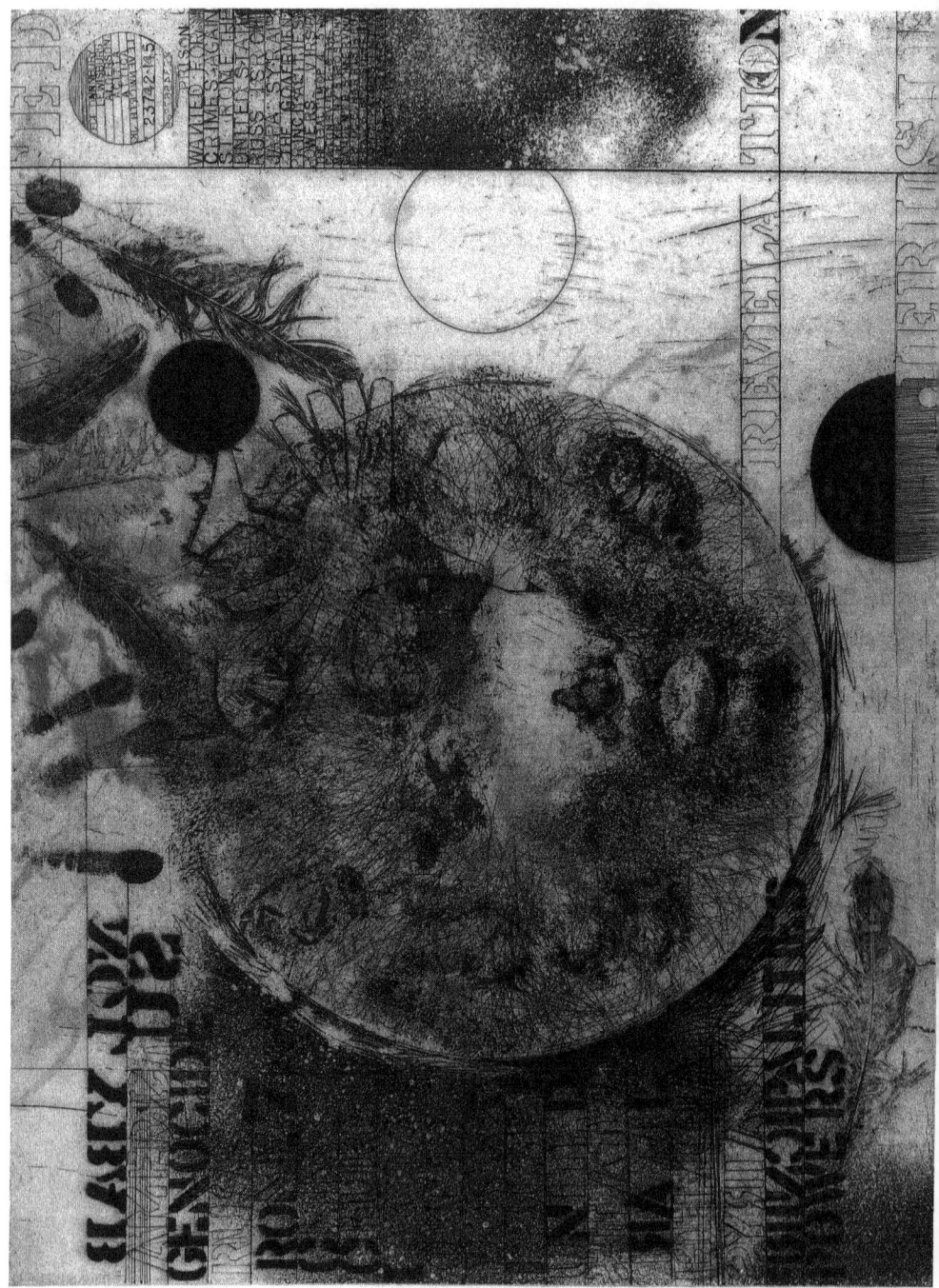

The Nightmare of God:
And How He Awakened

It is instructive and sobering at once; a book that begins on a visionary note, shortly slips its moorings, continues on a nightmare track. It all finally ends — who is to say how? — with a cannibal feast whose horror is scarcely assuaged by a levitated dream of new heavens, a new earth. Quite obviously not a comforting picture of human life, in whole or in part. Nothing platonic, synthetic. Rather, presages of disaster, tragedy, a fragmented series of images, hints, fits and starts; in sum, a dislocating book about a bad time. About our time?

Indeed, we are hard put to find "good news" in such a book. But could our quandary be — we look for such news where it is hardly to be found? Either our definition is awry, or we are magically inclined or culturally blinded; in other words, not free as yet to believe in the way the book invites. Rightly, we expect bad news from the world, and good news from the Gospel. The trouble being, the difficulty of distinguishing good news from bad. Must the bad news always precede the good? Must the bad news always be the real news?

To the believer, the Book of Revelation is good news because it speaks the truth (albeit strange, subterranean) about the world and history and the makers of history. It thus attacks our habitual way of thinking about ourselves, history, our place in the grand scheme of the world. Still, rigorously, it leaves us free: offering us an historic instance of one believing community, combating for its very soul with the imperial state. The book then advises: Judge your own time; this is how one community strove to be faithful.

Even this is not saying everything. The episodes wondrously tossed together in Revelation are (as we believe) "inspired." Thus they are elevated to the status of a sanctioned metaphor. Which is to say, God "stands by" this book — its community, the struggle it underwent, the decisions it took in confronting the state; more, what we would be inclined to dismiss today as its stiff-necked arrogance; in face of the devils that once stalked believers, in the days of belief. Nightmares, demons, mad horsemen, levitating angelic beings, they are all here, frightening, immensely real to the inner eye. But most of all, most blessed of all, most threatened of all — the community. God witnesses to it, offers its example to those who follow, as a way of freedom.

The ethic of that community is the fruit of ecstasy. Strange indeed. A revelation is granted. In its wake, believers stiffen their resolve; the slight wavering scrim between life and eternal life dissolves for this moment or that. But the conclusion is always a stern one: Jesus in glory, warns the community of its faults and blemishes. "I know your conduct." (Rev. 1:10) More, the revelation is first offered to an exile, a deportee, a forced laborer (a fairly constant situation for the prophet, the geography of his faith). Under such conditions does the voice of God become humanly audible. The Son of Man both unveils the mysteries, and formulates the conduct. He addresses the churches, approves, praised, threatens; He also underscores the promise — which is to become the life blood of these earthbound visionaries. "I know.... I approve!... I judge."

The Book is irreformably curious about events in the world; it is as though a gimlet eye were put to the outer dome of heaven. The view is encompassing, horrific, phantasmagoric. The tone is of sternness, exhortation, urgency. Earth is in trouble; human groupings have become parasitic, inhuman. The empire has its citizens by the throat. Old gods are dusted off for public showing. The state is not fooling around; worship its gods, or pay up. And the coinage is not a light one; the decrees are spelled out in blood.

These are momentous developments. Threatening to the strong, utterly demoralizing to the weak.

Humans have become empire makers and breakers. Every empire is summed up in Rome; and Rome is Babylon, that classical city of lawless grandeur. The church is warned: No ultimate trust is to be placed in the imperials arrangements. Otherwise, the church will be strangled at birth, and pass out of history with the bedizened fools and charlatans she courted.

More, the cultural matrix is dissolving. Neither land frontiers nor ethical belief nor a common language, hold firm. The question arises: How do believers conduct themselves in such a time? Consciousness, conscience, structures, all break up.

But the end of a culture is not necessarily the "end of things." The distinction is of import — for sanity, for truthfulness and sane and hopeful conduct. Signs of *some* end — whether the end of an era, a culture, an empire, are evident; something is falling away; signs of the essentially temporal, fragile character of human work, effort, genius, culture, are all about; a warning, a negative command. Right discernment of these signs is a kind of basic literacy testing of the faith. Are the Christians in touch with better, deeper, more reliable, harder won resources than mere citizenship in the empire? Let us say without a touch of cynicism, in a deeply serious way, they had better be.

Between the "now" and the "end," there is only the slightest of edges. The dust settles on human glory; today's political promise is tomorrow's horrid betrayal. Cynical? At least, Revelation offers an antidote, then and today, to the immense inflation of political rhetoric, the seizure of conscience by political gurus, reborn Christians.

The scriptural direction is something other than this; austere and devoid of cheap promise — for the millenarian and realist alike. Political forms, huge cultural puffing, the glory that was, the grandeur that will be — are these ever devoid of actual systematized violence?

A task therefore is implied: To place limits on what is an essentially unlimited political assault on the human spirit, the stalking beast of empire.

Limits must be placed on political questions. Indeed the term itself is often a cover, on the one hand for irresponsibility in citizens, on the other for a power grab. One has the right, indeed the duty, in the light of Revelation, to question the very term "political questions." Are they more than fabrications of latter-day tyranny, a distraction and denial of personal outreach, the replacement of the good Samaritan by the welfare state? Today's Christian, who has the advantage of a rather spotty Christian record in this regard, cannot but note the seductive, constant interloping of the state (including the Christian State) in the green pastures of Christian works, those of both mercy and justice.

Christians are thus served warning: Questions of literal life and death should not be reduced to merely political questions, posed and defined by the state, resolved by the state. Such a method only guarantees the inhuman treatment of humans, marks the dissolution of conscience before the onslaught of Big Brother. Today it is worth nothing that the state appetite grows and grows, no matter what the political arrangement: right, left or center. Questions that properly belong in the sphere of individuals or local communities are seized on from above, made the subject and object of political leverage; this happens in new parties and old, in manifestoes of Marxists, Catholics, fascists. New forms pretend to replace the old; inevitably they are forms of seizure and control; just like the old. Old or new, for Christians they only serve to justify the old cynical questions of Cain: Am I my brother's keeper?

Who is my brother? Who is to live? Who is to die? How is the earth to be allocated? Are we allowed to kill; and if so, in whose name, by whose authority? The questions cannot be answered by politicos or their myrmidons. For these are not political matters at all. Their seizure by politics, the vast broadening of political power represented by such assumptions, posed as matters of contention among power-hungry parties — this can only mean in the long run or short, that human needs are neglected, and humans degraded, narcotized.

It must be insisted in season and out, that the deepest questions of human life, those affecting communities, children, health care, education, these lie outside the competence of the state. The state has no right even to pose such questions, except to refer them back to the communities concerned.

Yet today, the state enters all these areas, boldly, with a full confidence in "its mandate," a mandate that lays claim on the progressive incoherence, cowardice and moral desperation of citizens. Into such a void, which is the void of modern conscience, rushes the state — armed with rhetoric, technology, a narcotic named death. One shot in the arm, euphoria followed by nirvana; one need never be concerned again.

Thereupon, surrounded by a sprawl of sleeping beauties, the state is free to move where, when, upon whom it will. It declares war, inducts the sleep-walkers, allocates (with its leftover goods and services) a stingy measure of medical care, housing, food. Some have access to this poor-house largess, most do not. Even in so-called "peace time" (a euphemism if there ever was one, our lives being constantly hustled between fevers and chills, hot war and cold) — the corporate state wastes the earth, dislocates minds, corrupts all areas of science, in its expanding military and economic adventurism. The earth itself grows too small, too puny for the weaponry that bristles from silos, proving grounds, bunkers. The people? The people be damned, they are seven times expendable; the computers have written them off by anticipation, hundreds of thousands of them, millions. And the earth? The earth also.

Bellicose, selfish, self-deluded, icy, absurdly resolute — behold the Rome of the Book of Revelation. Behold also America?

America: waging war as it does, preparing for ever more lethal incursions, power politicking, carving the earth into blocs, spheres of influence, like parts of a corpse. America: contemptuous of the precious accretions of civilization, culture, faith; enlisting all, resisting all. What is left for humans, what is left for Christians to do? We must resist the state.

Revelation of course does not teach that its appalling symbols, Babylon and Rome, offer a description of every state in history. The thought of say, citizens of Switzerland applying literally to themselves the exemplar of Babylon, is quite absurd. But the absurdity lies rather in the literal mind than in principled understanding. The Book of Revelation dwells on tendencies, hints, drives, directions, forces behind facades, the intent of underlying language, the gradual bending of minds, citizenship as *grand prix*, soul slippage, loss of a sense of mystery, captivation by omnivorous culture, dulling of conscientious edge, willing enslavement to death. Hints and signs for the spiritually literate spring from the book: the opening of the seals, the rushing horsemen, the trumpets of doom, the bowls of disaster, beasts and dragons at large; images all of them, of tendencies toward unmitigated violence and death, a kind of pandemonium of the rampant state, the rampant unregenerate spirit.

Every nation-state, by supposition, tends toward the imperial: that is the point. Through banks, armies, secret police, propaganda, courts and jails, treaties, treasuries, taxes, laws and orders, myths of civil obedience, assumptions of civic virtue at the top. Revelation in fact urges on us, in response to all this, a kind of Christian scepticism, in face of every political form and promise.

Still it should be said that of the political left, we expect something better. And correctly. We put more trust in those who show a measure of compassion. We agree, conditionally but instinctively, with those who denounce the hideous social arrangements which make war inevitable and human want omnipresent; which foster corporate selfishness, pander to appetites and disorder, waste the earth.

Thus we rightly feel betrayed when revolutions are succeeded by commissars, when vicious new tactics succeed the old. The point is worth stressing. There is certainly a social bias in the book of Revelation, in favor of the victims of social oppression. The bias, moreover, is in direct line with prophetic teaching. But the book also parts company with leftists or revolutionaries (just as it parts company with Caesar) whenever these undertake to announce the arrival of God's kingdom, by renewed violence and duplicity, to be sure. But inevitably (how often we have heard it), "in a just cause."

A constant tendency of politics in a time of social crisis is this: Everyone promises more than she or he can deliver. Everyone's politics is equated with the kingdom of God. The right grows as Pentecostal as the left, the old as loud as the new. It matters little after awhile that neither side, anywhere, is delivering bread-and-butter realities, simple justice. Regime after regime, in a desperate gamble for distracted following, or a desperate grab at the depleted earth, follows the most savage political methods, imprisons political deviants, suspends civil liberties "for the duration," tortures and executes its enemies, or supposed enemies, fails to liberate women, declares homosexuals and lesbians non-citizens, spies and bugs and surveys, degrades language through deceit and concealment.

We are, therefore, not to be taken in easily by claims and rhetoric. Nor to believe that the state, riding a moral hobbyhorse, speaking well of itself, has therefore become just or compassionate, or has eliminated poverty, or purged itself of racism or warmongering. Or in fine, has suddenly set blooming the garden of Eden; or announced the kingdom of God.

The church (ideally always, rarely in fact) has a word for such an entity; simply, "I am not you." — And that is resistance. I am not you. I deny your self-inflation. I deny your right over life, death, and conscience. I pierce your deception, propaganda, with the blade of the gospel. I confront your omnipotence with the greater power of nonviolence. Such a word to the state must in principle be heard in Sweden and Switzerland as well as in Ghana and Brazil and the USSR ... all across the world. In this sense, Revelation is archetypical; its symbols offer an instructional light to guide the Christian, under any and all forms of political life. Here it would mean a mild dissent, there, resistance unto death. The word of God draws a line, a line of light, a line of blood, if need be; hereby denying the state, always and everywhere, the right to proclaim itself savior, messiah, overlord, god almighty, alpha and omega.

Revelation denies also, pierces, deflates and unmasks what we might call the anti-symbols, those contrary to Revelation, the stolen ones. In our time certainly, these include the nuclear signs and wonders which proclaim, more powerfully than mere words, that the state bestrides the world, mounts the throne of absolute death, declares the time and place, and erects the machinery of the last day. No. Resist. Be the church.

It has been suggested that the book of Revelation is a thinly veiled political tract, laced with symbols that only the faithful community could understand, offering clues to political developments in the empire, hinting at the appropriate response of believers. According to this theory, Revelation arises out of political crisis; the book is a kind of broadsheet, published and passed around in the communities. It discusses Babylon where obviously it means Rome; talks about the Beast when obviously it means the Empire. It urges resistance on behalf of the beloved community, threatened in its first generation with brutality, torture, death, but also (and perhaps more dangerously), with painless intussesception, compromise, inclusion into the empire. All this, instead of following through on its painful destiny, "over against" empire.

All such theories aside, these themes form only a part of the book, preliminary to a necessary understanding of events, an exhortation to stand up in a bad time, to be accounted trouble maker. And this peculiar, uneasy stance of the church is something more than policy, good or bad; than politics, opportune or generous. The community of faith cannot *not* withstand the state. Resistance is a response to the sinful universe, as deep as metaphysic or nature. It is a response to the law of necessity, to a world that goes its own way. And woe to whoever stand in its way, in opposition!

Woe then to the church. She must be herself. The law that governs her sense of herself, and her consequent activity in the world, is this: She is a clue to the end of things, to the end of this or that era, to the end of the human adventure. Not a bang, but a whimper. But the return of the Lord. And meantime, fidelity unto death.

We could add this reflection about the present time. Human history (of which the empire is both pretentious subject and intoxicated author) slips its violent, absurd stereotype only in the light of Christ's return, His summing up — which is both judgment and illumination. Meantime, the church; sign and announcement of that return. She has nothing else to be or to do.

Still, the charade goes on; it is known as empire. Being itself, it is intransigent ("stuck" would be a less elegant but more accurate word for it). So, trouble is inevitable. Here and now, always and everywhere, trouble. The community stands there, blocking the hideous machine; its members look for all the world like Buddhist martyrs, serene, inward, utterly fearless. Their message is clear: Hands off! Hands off conscience, hands off the sanctuary, hands off the unborn, hands off the dying, hands off nonviolence. Hands off life!

Thus the church confronts the empire, with evidence of other power, other weapons, another sense of time. She is called to courage and patience, to cope with inhuman polity, to public decisions, to promoting the common weal, especially that diurnal "un-weal" of the poor and outcast.

All this perhaps sounds easy, in pulpits; or reads easy, on paper. In fact, it remains a terrible difficulty; how to be the non-state, the uneasy one, the perpetually unassimilated, the conscience, the unease of power, the victim, the minority voice. And this when everything in a given culture, a given state, would lead her down some woodbine path — toward disappearance.

The Nightmare of God

Indeed, from Rome to America, the empire shows a mordant genius for "including" everything, everyone, you, me, religion, in a suffocating imperial hug. Enfolding us in the Public Works Project Without Peer - which is to say, empire itself.

How stand up? With a sense, not of frenzy, but assurance, calm, self-awareness? The question here is not one of tactic or psychology. Believers are not called to meet this or that threat to their well-being (or their very existence) on terms of this world, tit for tat, violence for violence — or favor for favor. Such a church is merely contemptible, the sedulous ape of empire itself, its spiritual arm. And we have had enough of that — in Rome or Babylon or New York.

The Book raises another question entirely: the question of faith.

The promise: "He comes." The response: "Come Lord Jesus." The promise heartens the community for the struggle; just as the struggle helps it understand the terms of the promise. The two must go together, for the church is constantly tempted to strike bargains in high places, to declare a false peace with the world, to become no more than a debased and humiliated, though outwardly flamboyant, figurehead; a resource, an ornament, a unique, sought after, courted whore.

Revelation is thus a call to an austere, unworldly faith. The world is the arena of that faith; it is even a kind of bull pen, where martyrs are made or unmade — in more senses than one. In crisis as in worship, the church discovers Christ; the "Other," the non-emperor, utterer and keeper of promises, servant and sum of belief.

It is worth pointing out too that the last book of the Bible is remarkably consonant with the first, Genesis. There is a kind of second, final "naming of things" in Revelation, an effort to tell the truth, to speak of things as they are, to call crime crime, virtue virtue, to "call the shots" as they say; and this at a time when language is perverted to the debased uses of empire.

The naming is done mysteriously. Revelation is not the straightforward myth of Genesis; it is a box within boxes; a dream within dreams. Perhaps circumstances forbade a literal message, the author or compiler could not speak openly to the community. So his naming of reality, while profoundly truthful, is veiled.

Veiled or not, the truth is there. This community had recourse to the word of God, to the prophets that went before. Thereby, it spoke its own word, produced another chapter in the history of truth. And this, one cannot be reminded too often, at a time when the truth was all but drowned in a storm of propaganda and statist big claims.

The destruction of language! Orwell noted it as an onslaught of fascism on the native power of the mind. A sorrowful fact of life, ancient or modern. Its opposite number speaks in Revelation; the community and its book. In touch with truth, awakened to a taste for the truth, the believers turned to the world; there they spoke the unlikeliest and rarest of tongues: the truth.

Someone has said that the first casualty of war is the truth itself. For some fifteen years (the time period could be extended greatly) Americans have been victims of that loss. We have undergone an ideological assault on the mind's *power* over and *appetite* for the truth. In such a dreadful process the powers and dominations, idols and demons (Jesus and the Evangelists speak in different terms), keep the mind rocking, off balance. One recalls the Paris Peace Talks of 1972-73. Day after day, the news was a veritable seesaw. There will not be peace! There will be peace! Peace is at hand! Peace has escaped us! We have signed the accords; we have not signed. The war goes on; the war is over. And where was the truth?

Under such an assault, people become less and less certain that they can touch reality at all. They are cornered; they become convinced that the real world is no more than a concoction of power politics. The world belongs to others; "people like us" are simply powerless. Connection? Revelation? Response? Responsibility? My voice? A voice that can be heard, that counts for something? Meaningless. The world is created by the politically powerful and the rich, backed by military violence. The gods are enthroned; the world belongs to them.

Flayed by persuaders, hidden and overt, the people are disoriented and victimized. And not only the people; one must include here (the inclusion is seldom if ever made) the so-called brightest and best, the academic warriors who mislead, confound, alienate.

Another area Revelation opens up, a rich one indeed, is the world of signs and symbols. Signs of the end, signs of the present time. The symbols reach across time, offering a vision, leads, hints of what we are, what we are to become. Signs of the end, signs of the end time — such signs are discernible, as the community confronts the power of this world. "When he comes, will the Son of Man find faith on the earth?" Revelation does not attempt to answer the haunting question of Jesus; but it poses the question in a hundred voices, tones, signs, gestures.

Something else follows. Christians gathered in communities of faith, suffering, sharing of goods, sharing of risks, are in principle literate. They read the signs of the times. Christ has offered, not just an elevated version of life in the super state, a way of surviving there, but the truth about that life, the truth about citizenship. Thus we work through, ponder, renew and bring to life, symbols which nourish; symbols of faith under crisis, which reveal the empire's true intent, tooth and claw, the powers and principalities, the idolaters, world violence. Inevitably, strong elements of judgment infuse the signs. And more, a transcendent hope.

There is a wrenching irony here. The imperial state, that panoply of splendor and violence and worldliness, its immense outreach of moral disease, enticement, glory — the empire is ignorant of what it is, of the history it pretends to create. Its leaders are sleepwalkers. They know the uses (and misuses) of the imperial method; but of the needs and hopes of human beings, they are sublimely ignorant. Indeed, they are ignorant of the latter exactly in proportion to their skills in the former. And the citizens, as they become enlisted in the empire, and live off its fat and marrow (someone always pays), they too grow ignorant as they grow skilled. Wheelers and dealers, hangers-on, parasites, worshippers of the befouled gods of the state — all are deprived of the signs, the truth. Ignorant, enthusiastic covenant brokers and beneficiaries, leaders and led alike, alienated from house and bloodline. History simply escapes them. History is made elsewhere; in holes and corners, among mere survivors, dissidents, the burdens of conscience are borne, the weapons "that do not weigh one down." Thus the book of Revelation.

Clear lines are drawn. Indeed, why not draw them? At the least an effort must be made to clarify realities by way of distinguishing them. On the one hand brutal totalized violence, whose master image is imperial war. On the other, the ethic and conduct of the community in accord with the promise; in principal nonviolent, in principal willing to suffer rather than inflict suffering. Thus, the promise is honored, and its realization draws near. Indeed, the community is the realization of the promise, even as it draws strength from that source.

Such a view of things has immediate practical implication. Wisdom governs the community's view of citizenship; the believers are not easily gulled, taken in; they see the dizzy gap between political talk and performances. They have even measured the gap in practice; it widens like a hungry jaw, as imperial appetite grows; how anti-human, conniving and coercive the state authority can be. What a stereotype after all, how erratic, unventuresome in theory and fact; how neglectful of human need.

Such insights taken by themselves may of course be practically useless. Where do they lead? What is the dissenter willing to lay out? Is every idealist a sleeping child in a wakeful world? Is the defeated idealist only a full-blown cynic? One wonders whether distressing facts may not be as self-defeating as ignorance. In a period of social turmoil, despair is common and cheap, more common by far than courage, patience, self-renewal.

John must have known this. In the orbit of the Roman empire, many felt the hot breath of the imperial beast. Reformers, satirists, critics flourished. But life, as they say, went on. Justice was derided or denied, the poor were enslaved, violence flourished under the imperial banners; at certain levels of authority, the mighty stood outside the law. And the emperors, pretentious buffoons, had themselves declared gods. Absurdity crowned the work.

Even today, we experience the bestial fallout from all this, so much a part of our history that we repeat it with witless enthusiasm. In the first place, unlimited state violence utterly captivates the mind — the intelligent and skilled as well as the uneducated and poor. Who has not heard the cries, who has not repeated them; in one way or another, all are enlisted. Our country right or wrong! Love it or leave it! The diseased slogans are by no means shamed out of sight - by Vietnam crimes, by Watergate, by the shambles of American might in the world. Indeed, after all this, the limits of social violence appear as a kind of vertical counterpart of the old frontier myth — no limits in sight. Vietnam set the tone and pace and method; everything is permissible; unlimited killing, torture, destruction of hospitals and schools, the death of children. The facts of life are the facts of death.

Is knowing all this, realizing it, of value? Or does the knowledge petrify our resolve, overwhelm us with helplessness? An answer is not easily come on. But surely something further is required, something more than bad news, in order to make the times bearable.

The Book of Revelation recognizes this need. Telling the truth, naming things as they are, battling the empire with nonviolent weapons — if this is to occur, it must be joined to a promise. The promise offers meaning in the midst of social chaos — an outcome, a way out, a hope, a measure of compassion in the midst of runaway injustice. It is an abrupt interjection on behalf of life. "I return," a counter to senseless, abstract death. Such a promise invites the believer, half-drowned in the atrocious "facts of life," to discernment, to political resistance.

The Christian thus stands at the edge of the political maelstrom, a questioning mind, an outsider, a sceptic; simply because the promise is not verified, in principle cannot be verified, within political systems, within time and this world. Indeed, all concordats are discordant.

Then, a decision is called for. The Book of Revelation becomes "good news" in the basic evangelical sense, only in this hypothesis: that the community reading the Word is in resistance to the state, just as the community that first received the Word was in such resistance.

There is no other atmosphere or geography in which to receive this Word, except the one in which it first arose. Read in this stance, before the state, before the world, the book begins to make sense. The word finds its hearers, comes alive, becomes what it was meant to be, a handbook of resistance.

Could we be more precise about "resistance" as understood in Revelation? In what sense was the ancient community in resistance? Not merely as a political tactic, certainly. Rather, as a charism, a gift, a response to grace. Resistance was not a political response to intolerable political or social conditions. Rather, it was (and is) a conscious, believing opposition — a no, a refusal, a "not yet" uttered in the light of the promise of Jesus.

It implies a cool, long, askance look at a perennially unsatisfactory order of things; then, now, as long as time lasts; an order which even within its own definitions, is only spasmodically and unwillingly just, truthful only on occasion, compassionate only rarely. But this is not really the point. For the ultimate meaning of this dubious order is a claim; (and this cannot be stressed too strongly; it lies at the heart of the state's credentials, organization, the mystical hold it exerts on citizens). The claim is laid on all; it pretends, presumes to absorb and include all reality in its grasp. *L'etat, c'est Dieu.* The state is a principality indeed, the first of all that infesting multitude of spirits who claim us for their own.

Still, the empire's perennial inadequacy, duplicity, violence, does not exhaust the grounds for Christian resistance. Who would not resist such an entity, presuming rightmindedness, strength of character? But this is not the Christian basis for resistance. The believing community is not "over against," merely because the state is unjust. The heart of the matter is the state's claim to religious fealty. Quite simply, Christians are forbidden to worship idols. But the omnivorous state would embrace, enlist, all reality, including the church, including believers. Through taxation, through the military draft, a dragnet lies over all; the state cuts its lethal swath across all, silencing all, threatening all. When such a claim is yielded to, the idolatrous state stands self-justified. At that point also, the church has disappeared as "the other," the non-state.

This, it seems to me, is the *faithful* meaning of resistance; the recoil of faith upon idolatry. On eight or ten occasions in the book of Revelation, such faith is dramatized in the midst of resistance. A pause for worship occurs. A sublime moment, a held breath; the community both engages and enrages the idols. In worship of God, Christians refuse to worship the state. They show before the world the true stigma, the mark of being possessed of God. In so doing, they refuse once and for all to be stigmatized with the mark of the beast (which "mark," some say, was a symbol of military induction).

The Book of Revelation is "sealed"; sealing is generally thought of as a hindrance to knowledge. Here something more is implied: No one is *worthy* to open the book. Evidently we are back at our old question. Right thinking about history is first of all an ethical question; not an exercise, a problem-answer sequence; but a grace, a gift. He alone understands our history, its deep form and soul, Who has given Himself; "slain yet risen." Apart from Christ, the closure of the book is final, neither genius nor goodwill nor sane conduct avail to unseal it. Radical ignorance, anomie, alienation, are all but universal.

No one but God can open the book; because only He has closed it. Indeed, its entire subject is the holy One who opens the Book. No one else can decode it.

Indeed, only through Him (since through Him the unsealing takes place) can our blindness be healed. He is "standing as though slain." (Rev. 5:6) "He is worthy to open the book because he was slain and had redeemed us." (Rev. 5:9)

How live in the world as a believer? How discern, how discover, how unveil (re-velation)? The meaning of the world can never be known by men and women of the world; otherwise, all sorts of pelagian interventions, politics, five-year planning, economics, poetry, philosophy, would suffice, by now would have created both the meaning and the means of salvation, apotheosis, rebirth. What we have today alas, is something else; moral squalor, injustice, proliferated death; east and west, systems burnt out, malfunctioning ... the dance of death around the sealed book. No revolution has yet produced the "new" man — or indeed, the new woman.

The book (as will be revealed) is of divine origin, which is perhaps best translated as a record kept, and kept locked. But the book is not sealed forever. Locked in order to be opened, dramatically, by someone specially chosen, the Keeper of the book, its Giver Away, its Public Reader, its Loud Crier. Indeed, not the keeping of the book, but its unsealing, is the heart of the matter. Responsibility begins then, crime and punishment, the process, trial, error, judgment, history itself.

Inevitably, if history is to be defined not as a mill stream, a torrent, a speedy or slow current of time; but simply as judgment; then the unsealed book, the open book, will contain in its writing, in *actu primo*, all the following: crime, death, pathos, suffering, tragedy. A book about us. Therefore unregenerate, violent, criminal, godless even.

And yet it is God's book, known only to Him and to His faithful ones; in this sense, that even the criminals of history "do not know what they do"; the master minds are mindless....

The book is a Pandora's box. And it is Jesus who says: Let it all go, let it all happen. Every dog is to have its day; every horse and horseman.

Little by little, one by one, they come forward, strictly under control, on tight rein; not every Attila in one century; one Hitler at a time, one Vietnam, one horseman, one plague, a certain manifest, strongly-reined control. Not a pell-mell release of chaos into larger chaos, as in the myth of Aeolus and the winds, nor a foul expanding cloud of "ills and bads," as in the Pandora image. One by one, in a certain allotted space and time, with a measure of freedom; the horsemen come forth to attack, to subvert, to murder, to deceive; to be themselves (to be ourselves).

Things are bad, bound to be bad (unbound to be bad). But there is goodness too. Many will perish, the subversions of so-called good people, religious people, all but complete; for a time, for a space. Death will grow so inflated, so personalized, socialized, technologized, so totally in control of imagination, so possessive, so seductive; men and women will long for death; and death will escape them. (Rev. 6:16) Meantime, they adore the beast. (Rev. 13:4) For a time, for a space.

The horsemen of the book are personalized, become visible, public figures, once they are unleashed. The book is opened; it all hangs out; the unmasking of the principalities and powers. This is the work of Christ: to forbid evil its envied darkness. Evil would like to play its game behind the scenes; the argument that it does not exist rests on its invisibility. But Christ urges the forces out, prods them like beasts into the arena. Then the real contest, the one called history, can begin.

This we name, "calling the shots." The game is underway. In the bull pen, the beast without the antagonist makes no sense; nor does the hero alone on stage. Issues must be joined, if indeed there are issues. There must be a crisis if there is to be a drama. Forces are joined up close, a claim is leveled on conscience; call it draft, taxes, crime, war, even silence; they claim you, the look of a war poster. It is necessary therefore to disclaim, to disestablish, to resist. Even to die. Otherwise, the "second death."

Revelation is not a scripture, as commonly purveyed and preached — unless indeed it is a scripture of the damned. About us. About that body of Christ, which is His church, party to violence, partner to deception, whore, plaything, betrayer, seducer. And yet not entirely lost, since the "saints" also exist in her, are formed of her; also unmasked and released.

A secular book, therefore about God. A book about violence, therefore about God. A godless book, therefore about God. An historical work, a book about history, a book which is history itself, the only history, compressed and released, sealed and opened. About the world, therefore about God. Since He created the world (Rev. 4:11), since the One who opens the book is worthy to do so, since He has won a victory over the world. (Rev. 5:5) Since, indeed, He is its only outcome and hope.

The Book No One Could Open

A series of difficult, even outrageous images governs Revelation. Part of our history, part of western art — today we live with them uneasily, or not at all. The housebroken Christian imagination has all but given up on them. Add to that, the erosion of mind worked by technological folly; we stand light years from these immensely primitive, yet sophisticated images, of our fate, our damnation, our hope.

Today we assume that common sense is in the saddle. The horsemen, the seals, the dragons, cosmic women, gargantuan demons — we have ridden them out of town. Rational discourse! Coherence! We have bitten off a myth whole, peddled it, bought it, huckstered it, in place of the very truth. No matter that in public and private, the "new truth" is a very old madness, that it justifies murder and pushes the world to the brink. It is all done sweetly and confidently, in the name of the rational mind, in tribute to the good sense we so value.

Or do we?

The prophet John is of course directly at variance with this treppaned madness. His book lingers around the edge of the so-called rational method. The dwelling of truth, he protests, is not what you assume it to be; it has crevices and corners and dark nooks and crannies unreachable by your fine-honed intellects. And the spaces you cannot touch — they are far from empty. Living creatures, busy and playful, demons and angels, terrors and ecstatics, movement and stillness, the living, the so-called dead, all dwell there — in your dwelling. Your soul is a haunted house, as is your world. And you take no account of it; in a strange mix of arrogance and dread, you turn your back, take up your pocket calculator; and think to tote the dimensions of the real world.

Real world! Reality presses upon you; unreality is driving you mad.

A creeping apocalypse (no longer creeping, a torrent, a wild fire) is out, in the open. Demons occupy the house, seven times renewed, strengthened, secular, violent, skilled, on the move. An ersatz salvation, the imperial nation as God almighty, war its hideous liturgy. In Revelation, the myth of the "rational mind" in touch with a "reasonable world," encounters full face — the imagination, the alternative, judgment on the "modern," the "real," the "relevant," all that silly list of suppositions and stopgaps. Can the imagination, the very method and substance of the book, exorcise that jumble of myth and dark hope and selfish grasp, the statistics, body counts, charts and figures, gross products, rational inventions? Can the mind, wearied and weakened before a world it can no longer grasp, a rampage of modern horrors, yield before the prophetic nightmare?

That nightmare is truer than the truth. The imagination of John has taken the measure of the world, shown who we are, what we are about, beneath and beyond the frantic effort to render reasonable the waking horror in which, willy-nilly, we toss about like disintegrating dolls. We resist; we want control, even of a nightmare; we want to wrestle it to the ground, win the mastery, open the secret chambers, the abyss, posses and inhabit it. And it all gets nowhere. Every fresh assault, every new plan, only serves to worsen things. Absurd hopes fester away; they become more absurd as their realization becomes more improbable. Every five-year plan of church and state, from Detroit to Moscow, goes up in smoke; men and women are flattened to ground under the eager wheels of "social progress," "development," "wars on poverty."

"Our sickness must get worse...." A nightmare is in progress. Four horsemen, seven seals, the plaint of the innocent dead, the despair of the guilty living — finally, "silence in heaven for half an hour." (Rev. 8:1) We are well advised, for the sake of soul and sanity, to listen — and to grow silent.

The first horseman holds a bow, a crown is given him; he is already triumphant.... "He went out in conquest (conquering) that he might conquer...." (Rev. 6:2) The atmosphere is of an irresistible force, self-assured. He is not to be stopped, there is no evidence that he will be. He exults, radiates the persuasion of a further victory, a victory already achieved.

But who is this winner, conqueror, prevailer? Several details are worth noting in his regard. His horse is white. The color sums up, draws to itself all the hues of creation. And the rider is not only the first to be unleashed, "unsealed" — he is the unique one, the one in command of the others. He leads, gives direction and tactic and command.

He is also in opposition.

Further, he "holds" the bow. But the crown is "given him." A weapon is in his hands, but no indication is offered as to its use, in contrast to the other riders. The bow lies inert, slung across the shoulder and breast. May we not connect the bow, then, with a very old biblical notion, the "bow in the clouds," a sign of covenant? Only in this case, the bow is no longer in the heavens, it lies across the body of one who goes forth "a conqueror to overcome."

No hint of battle. He is not a warmaker, he is a maker of peace. All the Scythian warriors in the world (so dear to commentators) will not provoke him to string that bow. It is not the first time a weapon has become a symbol of peace. Indeed, the curving arc, the tension, the relative weightlessness of the bow make it an apt symbol of that unbroken once-spoken word of God, a promise: "No more will I destroy the earth by flood." (Gn. 9:11) Now the promise is renewed: "I come." Literally, One carries the promise. And only One. By whom is it to be borne, this weight of glory, if not by one who conquers plague, war, hell itself, leads them like lackeys, forward into history — to do their damnedest? After all, to do only what is strictly allowed, to be restrained, under scrutiny; to raven about the world, always and everywhere under the scrutiny of One who knows, sees, compassionates, judges; who is Himself outcome and meaning and crown of all....

"Conqueror, He went forth to conquer." There could hardly be a more marvelous, skillfully syncopated phrase to express the dynamism, the rhythms, the resolved and unresolved ironies of history, the knots of death thrice tied and untied, the work of Jesus, once and for all achieved (the cry from the cross; "it is achieved"), the terrifying bloody stew of the world, the cry of injustice, the death of the innocent; finally, the inscrutable silence of God. Has He done anything on our behalf, has He made any difference at all? More to the point, do our lives, stuck as we are in the bloody track of modern life, make any difference? "He overcame, he went forth to overcome." We may confess a passionate ignorance of the meaning of the phrase, an indignation even; it lies like a stone in our path, a scandal. We look up from the page of the Bible, the world meets our horrified gaze. What a world! And God claims a place there? Not only a place. He claims to be in command, to ride roughshod over the criminal, the unjust, the killers and torturers. Claims to ride first. An image of gravity, of place and time. An image moreover of eminence; He is literally the first energy of all truly human movement, its impulse and soul. And in regard to those sinister godlike outriders who follow; He claims to be in charge of them, commander of that hideous troika; they must move at His pace, right or left at the twitch of His bridle.

It is all too much. Our expectations fall, brought down at a stroke. This noisome world is no scandal to us; we are inured to the stench of death. But what of God? How can He thrust such an image at us, an outrageous image, one that simply does not correspond to the facts of life? Now if He only came toward us as beggar, orphan, cripple, holocaust victim, starving peasant.

But a conqueror! It boggles us, even (as we say) with the best will in the world.

It must be said, in the first place, that no single image of Revelation (or of New Testament symbolism) exhausts the reality of Christ. To speak of Revelation alone, there are images of another order entirely: the one clothed in a bloody robe, the lamb who is slain. In this way, through multiple images, contrasting, shocking, a balance is kept, between the unutterable tragedy of His mortal life, and the conquest indicated through the horseman image. How else indeed, except by a barrage of opposite energies and ironies is John to bring together the depths and heights, the journey and end-time, the cosmic and personal, the death and victory of this one called the Christ? In another place (Rev. 5:5-6), he offers perhaps the most daring juxtaposition of all: The lion of Judah is announced by one of the holy elders at the throne. John turns and beholds not a lion, but a lamb. Extremely disconcerting, a stroke of genius! From such a visionary, one can expect only the unexpected.

But as to our first horseman; he wears a bow of covenant, but he is given a crown. (The Greek text is precise; active voice, then passive.) He himself is covenant and promise; but his victory over the dead is an act of God. Still, the crown and bow befit. They are parallel accouterments. It is by his refusals, by his nonviolence, that the Lord prevails; "worthy is the lamb who was slain, to receive all honor and glory...." (Rev. 5:12)

If only the second, third, fourth horsemen could learn! But they are literally blind. Through all time, they remain simply themselves, sublimely, dreadfully so. They are like the stone warriors on some classical pediment; they plunge and rear and radiate a horrid energy. But they get nowhere. Thus while the progress of the first horseman announces the sovereignty of spirit over violence and terror and duplicity, theirs is simply a rampage — violence, terror and duplicity.

We should not miss the altogether astonishing though sorrowful irony implied here. First comes Christ; first in rank, a spirit of salvation. Straight as an arrow from His bow of fire, an unvarying moral continuity in the world. Then the other three. They plunge out blindly, each veering in his own direction, blindly in pursuit of prey. Each presumes himself the only force in the world, the only one riding the saddle of time, a Napoleon, an Attila, a Cyrus, a Caesar, a Pharaoh; truly each is a booming boring stereotype; see one, see them all. But with respect to the first horseman: implacable opposition, a battle to the finish. Who shall own the world, in whose name, by whose will is history to go forward? The three know; or think they know. In our name; which is to say, in my name, second, third, fourth. Their dark minds are exactly calibrated to the same destiny, each of them is a dark cloning of the other; spiritually speaking, they are programmed robots. They differ only in the color they bear, the color they would paint the world: pale death, red violence, black hunger. Take your choice, the choices are not large. What they offer is what they inflict, they have only one product to huckster, one world to posses. It is called death.

Thus in John's vision, history unfolds in two directions, not one. But we are not to be deceived. He is not teaching the dualism of the pagans, modern or ancient. The moral process of the world is not reducible to good versus evil, equally matched, outcome in doubt. No. All appearances to the contrary, the three mounted brigands are slaves and captives, hostages of the first. For all their freewheeling and exulting, they are strictly reined in. They are in fact little more than animated mimes, for all their cries of liberation, of human development, of armed struggle, of guns in good hands, of just wars, triage and the rest. Let them cry, let them go, let them win. They will not go far, nor forever.

The second warrior bears in addition to a sword, an explicit commission. His instruction: to enlarge the scope of violence; his orders: to pluck peace from the earth.

And the question arises: can God confer a mission to violence? We can only say haltingly, in fear and trembling, He offers a commission to the violence of nonviolence; that is, to the unmasking of violence, the acceptance of consequences, the weight and burden and malice of violence coming down on one's life.

The Nightmare of God

But in what sense can God be said to loose violence so brusquely upon the earth? Are these warriors human, superhuman, subhuman — or are they no more than allegorical figures?

Let us not complicate things. It seems as though at some periods of history (I would venture, at almost any period) violence reaches such a horrid peak as scarcely to be laid to any imaginable human elements. Violence then speaks for itself. Beyond its presence and method, no justification exists, or can be called for; it is irresistibly persuasive. It goes its way; too bad for humans. One need only think in this regard of the stunning power of war, once it is underway. Woe to the hapless who in the midst of the smoke and confusion, insist on thinking for themselves. Why are we here? Who is the enemy? Why must I die? The questions are inadmissible. The violent myth is in command.

Such a questioner, such a noncombatant, is a human illustration, the best one I know of, for the activity symbolized here. God, like this resister (or the resister, being godlike) places Himself at a deliberate, cool distance from the conflict. And raises questions. The service, humanly speaking, is a magnificent one; a "demyth" to counter the noisome, bloodthirsty, self-deluded myth that obscures the war, even while it thirsts for more blood.

Thus evil unleashed is also unmasked. Forces long hidden, all the more malevolent because hidden, passions, drives, hatreds, once simply invisible, are now "unsealed."

> *Immediately another horse appeared, deathly pale, its rider was called Plague, and Hades followed at his heels. They were given authority over a quarter of the earth, to kill by the sword, by famine, by plague and wild beasts.* (Rev. 6:8)

The summary is of intense interest. Today, we are told, famine and pestilence have been banished; that is the rhetoric of the first world. They are in fact banished only in the first world, and even there, only within the severest boundaries set by race, self-interest, income. The dollar stakes out the area of immunity from death.

Today, roughshod, unchallenged, war advances to seize the place, the power formerly assigned to these others, famine and plague. A dominant metaphor, war supplies the energy and insight for so-called advances against famine and disease; out of war come technical medical skills, instruments, a kind of backhanded tribute of death to life; a strictly extracurricular benefit, to be sure.

But in Vietnam, as well as in Laos and Cambodia, war brought the conquest of disease and hunger to an abrupt halt. It even revived them, set them in motion once more; strictly in its own service. We bombed hospitals, leper colonies, released defoliants which seeded cancer in tissues; we destroyed crops, rendered huge land areas unarable, bombed the dykes. It was a cost-benefit decision of considerable genius; what need of four horsemen, when one will do? No need of four to quarter the tortured earth, a corpse on a slab. One gargantuan fire breather, aloft in the heavens, bestriding the earth, a carnivorous charger and master. Death, famine, pestilence? Let them be his subalterns, his bully boys.

The fifth unsealing is a scene of strictly cold comfort. The victims wait in a kind of limbo, in contrast to the freewheeling progress of the mounted killers. The faithful dead are detained, closed in, lodged in a kind of prison, waiting. More: they are complaining. How long will the horseman ride? When will you render us justice? The answer is not comforting. "There are still more of you to die. Wait." History being what it is, the horsemen are still abroad. They will ride as long as time lasts. The swath they cut, its breadth and length, is the very roadbed of history. So be patient. There will be no justice until all accounts are in. Wait, your brothers and sisters must join you.

The first four seals restrained mythical creatures, embodiments of social evil. The fifth is about reality, the dead, those who have perished in service to justice. And something astonishing occurs. They will not stay dead, they take voice; their conscience, unfinished business in the world, their pain, are heard from. (They are not to be thought of as "the damned," the "second dead," who would have no interest in questions of justice.)

Do they have interest for us, that we might share this destiny: to live for others, to die for others? This scene is a very linchpin of Revelation. At the still point of death and defeat the holy ones refuse to be silenced. They want simply to know why they died. Why the world broke them. Why the kings and colonels won. Did such questions arise in their mortal days? Did they have time to voice their plaint? In any case, in a kind of limbo of obscurity and isolation, "beneath the altar," they raise the question, a question of existence itself.

They remind us of something infinitely precious. Conscience unstifled, unsilenced, unsatisfied, is the only reality that follows us into eternal life, the only evidence that our lives on earth have continuity and outreach; their lives with ours, time with eternity, all lives with each life. A cry for justice, for vindication. If we are conscious at all, we know that the cry is not heard, is only half heard, given an answer of sorts. But still unheard in this world, even in the case of the martyrs. And in eternity, cold comfort. The appeal is heard; it is not granted. Patience is recommended, the echo across the void of justice denied; but the echo also of a vivid sense of justice unstifled.

Indeed, this fifth seal seems to burst open to a dread accompaniment; something like a hideous body count. Is this the only meaning of the mournful history revealed here? We know it is not. More is to come; in the light of that promise, a promise of death transfigured, the plaint of the martyrs is bearable. History, we are told, culminates in the lives of the martyrs. Even after death, they are assured only of more death; the horsemen will ensure, with the their cold murderous progress, that the martyrs will never lack company. The martyrs continue to die.

Thus tragedy and promise are fused. At the same time, the bloody pretensions of the horsemen are defeated; their seizure of time, peoples, history. The tyrants are in fact only the base instruments of the providence of God. Meantime, in time, in this world, no word of vindication. Strange? Let us suggest only at this point (for the difficulties raised are thorny, and require more space) that the heroic dead are their own vindication, those who make up the measure of the suffering of Jesus in their own bodies, the "pleroma," the completion of the body of Christ.

Ourselves? In any case, the very name of time is patience. They were told to wait "a little while."

The Vietnamese said to us who visited their country in the midst of their torment: "Patience is a revolutionary virtue." In contrast, the time sense in the Western culture is wrong, awry. For us, time is impatience. It is the impatience of the machine. It recognizes only results, "solutions" to suffering and injustice — solutions which, it goes without saying, invariably go nowhere.

The dead end of this mentality is of course military. The war machine offers the final, efficient, fast solution to conflict and human difference; that is to say, extermination.

And one thinks, once more, of Vietnam. In the measure that the Buddhists, those with a millennial tradition of nonviolence, resist the machine (the war machine), and so vindicate the person, the community, their own tradition — in this measure, the center of world gravity will shift, west to east. The Vietnam War indicated this event is imminent, if it has not already happened. Those who wish to join the future reject the machine. This means that we face up to a spiritual difficulty; for the machine permeates our consciousness, our way of regarding one another, our way of regarding the planet. Many of us are interiorly militarized; mobilized in service to the culture, immobilized with respect to the person. Our time sense is wrong. The biblical time sense, "a little while," so often referred to by John, is nearer the Eastern millennial sense, the sense also of the psalmist, than it is to our murderous impatience.

The community of Revelation is evidently gifted with the charism of prayer. The gift grants insight into the iron march of time, the stereotype of power irresistibly in motion. The community has its own time piece, which is, after all, what Paul calls "the mind of Jesus." A perspective, a self-distancing from the fury, the big persuader. In this view, the perspective of a faith that sees further, sees that all time is but a "little while." This is true not because time, history, human life are unimportant. And certainly not because one is allowed to opt out of suffering, or ignore the penalties awaiting the conscientious. No, the "little while" makes sense only in light of the promise; it renders all pain, all loss, all human grandeur and pretension relative, de-deifies them, loosens their hold on the soul. All things good, all things a sign; but one Thing better, one a final reality.

"Wait a little while." Patience is the response of God to the importunate cry of the saints. Evidently, the response is no "answer," nor is it meant as such. What it offers, is merely to cast the question in a new light, to lead the mind deeper into the implication of its own anguish. "How long must we wait until you vindicate our death?"

Can we avoid putting such questions to God? We cannot expect less of God than we do of human authority. If the most we can hope for from earthly justice is mere moments, occasions, exceptions, rather than a continuum of justice (or at least, a sense that there exists in those who dispense justice a sense of quandary, a modicum of compassion), if indeed a "system of justice" is a contradiction in terms, then we have every right (every duty in fact) to expect more of God. Will He right human wrong? Is there a karma somewhere down the road? Even if we cannot see the end of the road, is the end, the illumination, the moment of truth at least promised?

Questioning God, given the moil and toil of the world, seems in fact to make some remote sense. He alone can be brought to this bar. We throw up our hands; who else will answer us? The lesser demand (in fact, the valid demand, the passionate demand) for a measure of justice, for a limit on injustice, for clearsightedness about crime and criminals, all this must hang in the air. "You were right in crying out." How could one live in the world, and not cry out? The "Holy and truthful One" to whom the dead make appeal, alone transcends the inhuman system that has ground them to bits.

The just who raise their cry, dwell "under the altar." (Rev. 6:9) Their death is one with His sacrifice. This is their glory. Still, for a time, for the time that fuels their cry, they remain without vindication.

The ultimate injustice worked against them is, of course death. Death was inflicted on these patient, sublime, impatient heroes, by the state. After "due process," as they say. The death of the martyrs is thus the ultimate injustice, the crown and capstone of the crimes of history. And against it, there is no appeal, no hope of vindication in this world.

It is not that one is forbidden to appeal to human courts, in an effort to resolve one's plight. But in a just cause (even in an unjust one) one must be prepared to be treated unjustly, as a plain matter of course. Even to be put to death.

Moreover, there is no divine interference, no saving miracles; as there were none in favor of His Son. Jesus is vindicated, the Father raises Him from the dead. But death preceded the act of God.

Still, the question resonates on the air of this world: Why do we suffer fruitlessly, unreasonably, unjustly? We cannot stifle the question, cannot "act as though" the sovereign conscience of God erased our own. Indeed, the one who has not been touched by, burned by the injustice of this world, doled out so prodigally by church and state; such a one knows nothing of the appalling silence of God.

It is unthinkable that such a question would not be a constant one, riding the air of the world, arising from every place; a sense of outrage, a sense that things could be, should be different.... The questioning of God is a mode of true faith in God.

In my vision, when he broke the sixth seal, there was a violent earth-

quake and the sun went as black as coarse sackcloth; the moon turned red as blood all over, and the stars of the sky fell on to the earth like figs dropping from a fig tree when a high wind shakes it; the sky disappeared like a scroll rolling up and all the mountains and islands were shaken from their places. (Rev. 6:12-14)

In Revelation there is a kind of ecological solidarity with crime and punishment inspired by the "day of wrath" symbol. God avenges; He is not patient forever; "all finally, go hide themselves in the rocks and caves" (Rev. 6:15) (We have an ironic parallel with the later experience of the hermits and cenobites, who also hid out; in order to find God, not escape Him.)

What has become of our dream, where did it go sour? Where are the magic "normal times"? A more absurd, unverifiable phrase cannot be thought of. Normal death, normal exploitation, normal consumerism. The absolutely abnormal, by a monstrous sleight of hand, a degradation beyond words, calmly walks on stage, seizes the main role, announces itself as the very model and paradigm of the human.

But not forever, Revelation declares. The abnormal, the reign of death, is finally unmasked. The Day of the Locust, the Day of the Bomb, Doomsday.

Peculiar to Revelation is the enumerating of those who flee the horsemen, the cosmic catastrophe. The scene is naive and terrible at once. The plaint of the martyrs, if not vindicated, is at least given weight and credence; the oppressors and murderers are confounded. The wheel of justice, on which the innocent and valiant had been broken, turns once more; only now, it is the great ones of the earth who are bound to its spiked circumference.

Who can read of such things, without a tremor of dread possessing his spirit? It is as though the whole earth had been transposed in the image of Cain. Evil, fecund and vile, generates more evil.

The faithful dead have perished at the hands of the three horsemen, victims of their malign power. Then the disoriented uncoping mob is set loose by the sixth seal, a contrast to the serene plaint of the faithful. Almost two species of humanity are thus presented. The latter, the conscientious, suffer the consequences, although they are marked ironically with a seal of divine protection. Then stream forth the despairing, those whose violence and selfishness are now unmasked; who lived for themselves, who die unto themselves.

They call out, these desperate ones, not to God, but to the very elements of the disaster that dogs them. They worship and welcome death; they "pay tribute to one they have failed to pay tribute to." (Rev. 6:16) Are these the words of Cain, or of the sons and daughters of Cain, the tribe of the unregenerate, the despairing? In any case, a kind of hideous recognition scene, just before the sky falls in.

Or from another point of view, is the scene only a grand illusion, the perennial dream of the enslaved and violated and persecuted of this world, another narcotic for losers?

It may be. Or again, it may be something more: an image of comfort — delayed indeed — but still, a hint of justice, a millennium not forever beyond our grasp.

Meantime, a few reflections occur.

There is no justification for the view that the sins of the great are judged in this world. Quite the contrary. The great, thank you, in their corporal frames or out, do quite well; ambitions are rewarded, honors conferred; then, state funerals, public bronzes.

As far as we're concerned, who purportedly march to a different drummer, our prayer is not that the great perish, but that they be converted. The Bible texts which refer to justice are in God's mouth, not ours; their fate is in His hands, not ours.

Also, a biblical sense of justice ought to include rehabilitation, not punishment. Otherwise, we merely reflect the punishing skills of this world — stale, vicious, futile as they are.

Finally, even when we seek justice, vindication, restoration of moral balance in a given community, the granting of our prayer may well include both the charism of patience and further suffering in the community. Let the one who prays beware! The prayer may be answered. Are we ready for surprising answers to perfectly just plaints and questions?

> *Then all the earthly rulers, the governors and commanders, the rich and men of influence, the whole population, slaves and citizens, took to the mountains to hide in caves and among the rocks.* (Rev. 6:15)

Believers are conspicuously absent here. Are they spectators of the fury? Are they exempted from its swath? Or is the scene only the outer sign of an inward damnation, a theatre of cruelty and absurdity, playing itself out in the masks of the great? In any case, the kingdom of this world suffers no exception; all are guilty, all are in flight. In the great empire from Babylon to Rome, all designations based on status, skills, class, income, are struck down; useless, utterly irrelevant. Disaster; the great are ignominiously toppled. What matter now honors and distinctions? No more rich, powerful, captains, nobles; all are poor and powerless, authority is wrenched away, every face is degraded, ignoble, racked with dread.

Now too it is clear. The slave was not a slave; he or she made decisions, he or she allowed herself to be enlisted in the criminal state. And the "free man" was self-deluded; he or she was free only to be criminal. Now, hiding, fleeing, they call out to a god they cannot bear. They are the self-condemned, finally paying tribute to those who believe, in spite of all. Judgment is at hand, that supreme reversal of roles in which God delights. It is a *magnificat* in the mouth of the damned. His arm achieves the mastery; He routs the haughty and proud of heart; He puts down princes from their thrones and exalts the lowly; He fills the hungry with blessing, and sends away the rich with empty hands.... (Lk. 1:51)

The Nightmare of God

How does this seal connect with the preceding one? Those who flee ignominiously, the hideouts, the uprooted, are the gentlemen who command the three horsemen. They breed, train, feed horses, and hire the riders — the most skillful and daring available. They wield the power that keeps the plagues raging through the centuries. From the point of view of time and this world, of history as commonly understood and written, they are the winners; their bets are sure, their return incalculable. But in all this extraordinary show, this pretension, this seismic shift of civilizations, personalities, military genius, eloquence, the persuasiveness and brutality that literally move mountains, in all this huffing and puffing, the truth emerges: They are subject to God.

He tells the truth. He unmasks. He raises up and brings down. He limits the power of death in the world. He levels pretensions, reverses roles; thus He grants even to the damned the truth of their existence. A gift, a bitter gift; who else grants them the truth, the truth of their crimes?

Thus the fate of the tyrants named plague, war, violence, famine, racism, sexism. In the world they went by pseudonyms; they were named political adjustment, power, Realpolitik, foreign service, military service, diplomatic service. Now God names them — for what they are. And the naming is a terror.

Unsealing, unmasking, revealing, these are offices of the truth, of God. Need one add, of ourselves? Evil is most itself, most entrenched and confident, when it is concealed. Modern techniques of concealment, decked out in the paraphernalia and myths of high office, include in the nature of things, a self-justifying rhetoric, a cover of untruth. We have perhaps seen enough of this in recent years.

It goes without saying that scripture offers something other than this unsavory arrangement, the opposite of untruth, of ideological nonsense, of myths of ego and self-esteem.

Let us also add: The unmasking of the Big Lie is a characteristic Christian activity in bad times — or ought to be. In good times, the truth is in the air, accessible to people who seek the intentions of their leaders (or want to replace their leaders). Indeed, is this not a workable definition of "good times"? And judging the times by such a standard, modest and workable, would it not be accurate to say that none of us can remember the last time he or she was "visited by good times"? When did we not feel deranged, kept outside the closed minds and stale corridors of power, denied access to the political game? We are like the dump-pickers in a poor republic; we spend our days on the city garbage, looking for a nugget or relic or remnant of the truth. Lucky we, if we come on a single page of scripture. like a Dead Sea Scroll, half obliterated by weather and neglect and age, offering us a "word of life."

Bad times indeed for the great society? But in just such times, we are told, God the Unmasker strips evil of its mask and enchantments, "calls it like it is" in the inelegant, telling phrase. Even through us, who ponder the word, as best we can, and now and again, act faithfully? Come Holy Spirit.

The Lamb then broke the seventh seal, and there was silence in heaven for about half an hour. (Rev. 8:1)

This is the silence which precedes and announces a momentous historical event.

The unsealing is a sublime counterpoint, brief, ineffable, a "silence in heaven." A climax, the denial of all necessity, death, action and passion. Not passivity, not the frozen inner circle of hell. But Dante's "ingathering of the rose." Presumably, we understand the other unsealings; it is all our history. But what of the silence here?

Can we sense that the interstices of silence in the history of the world, in the gospel, in the history of Christianity, are the very preludes to eternity? This silence is a clearly defined intercession in the turmoil, chaos, death, suffering, announced by the six prior actions. All that is past; now there is silence; no message, no media.... The silence in heaven celebrates those who make no mark in history or time; those who went unheard because of neglect or indifference; the nameless peasant, the body count, those who went down without a cry. Also the great contemplatives: those who choose silence; those who are chosen for silence; unknown lives, uncared-for deaths.... Then the silence of Jesus, His intermittent desert silence, the silence of His nightlong prayer to the Father, immediately before choosing the disciples, His silence before Herod. He has nothing to say to the powers of this world. They may seize Him. It is all on the record; to add would be to subtract. He does neither. At the end, a massive dignity, a weight of the Spirit lies on His witness and words, on the death that is imminent. The silence of His death is broken only by the great cry of resurrection.

> "It would represent a vital breach in the technological society, a truly revolutionary attitude, if contemplation could replace frantic activity.... 'Contemplation is the key to individual survival today; an attitude of profound contemplation allows actions to redeem their significance and to be guided by something other than systems and objects.'" (Octavio Paz)

> "If you would be genuinely revolutionary in our society (I repeat that I am not disclosing an eternal truth or a permanent value), be contemplative; that is the source of individual strength to break the system." (Ellul)

In this sense, the contemplative overcomes — overcomes the culture. This remains true, though the culture is also able to ape contemplation, as the beast can ape God. By "bending" contemplation also to its own uses and needs, psychologizing experience, so that men and women literally are flayed alive, have no skin left to live in the world and take its blows. By sexualizing experience, inflating pleasure at the expense of the responsibility, the longevity and patience of love. By politicizing experience, persuading us that all questions of welfare, community, individual development, right use of the earth, are to be solved "within the system"; thus rendering the system an absurd idolatrous tribute, binding our alternatives to a procrustean bed. And finally, by brutalizing experience, setting up implacable enmities, distant and obscure, which we are required to accept on our leader's word. How often we heard it, during the infamous Vietnam decade: Trust your leaders; they know more than you. Such enmities, prodded into inflammation by "leaders who have become misleaders" pollute our souls; we know ourselves only through our hatreds. Hatred, ice and fire, fever and chill becomes the temperature of humanity.

There must be another, better way. In silence, it may be granted to us.

The Day After Doomsday

> *Next I saw seven trumpets being given to the seven angels who stand in the presence of God. Another angel, who had a golden censer, came and stood at the altar. A large quantity of incense was given to him to offer with the prayer of all the saints on the golden altar that stood in front of the throne; and so from the angel's hand the smoke of the incense went up in the presence of God and with it the prayers of the saints. Then the angel took the censer and filled it with the fire from the altar, which he then threw down on to the earth; immediately there came peals of thunder and flashes of lightning, and the earth shook.*
> (Rev. 8:2-5)

The liturgy is instructive. There is an element of ascent, tranquil prayers go up, incense is offered, then comes a majestic moment: the casting to earth of the fire from the altar. As though to say, this is the way with true liturgy; it burns, it shakes the earth, causes thunders, voices, lightnings, tremblings. A passionate will is expressed: to connect the divine with the terrestrial, the human and the heavenly. God is fire, and the fire falls to earth. There is also a kind of unsealing, a trumpeting of evils to follow.

> "The most impressive fact of all is that this eschatological pause becomes an act of worship; in the midst of the turmoil of the terrible events of the last days, suddenly there appears this oasis of worship and adoration. ... God gives to his own the possibility of a worshipping stillness, from which the prayers of the saints, as the sole earthly element, rise to heaven. Thus the communion of prayer with their heavenly Lord is always possible, when all other earthly help is vain...." (Lilje, *The Last Book of the Bible*)

The "myth of explanation" was a false assumption from the start. God does not explain Himself or the universe, in the common way of theology. He simply offers us a myth; seals, trumpets, bowls. Thus a primitive method raises a question: Are we not to understand human life, as something other than a static "given," as the actual mess we are going through? ...

It might be said that Revelation offers an older, "religious" way of understanding; it turns out to be the most highly charged with secular understanding of all; that is, it takes the terror into account, the beast, the seven catastrophes, the *shekinah* of disaster overhead, the mythologies, the obsessions, untruths, seductions — the world in fact and its horror — and it offers a way out.

Today we are reportedly in a more chastened frame of mind. Things go badly, the world is after all unmanageable. And the least controlled elements of the runaway world are our own hearts. Consequently, the symbols of Revelation, dismissed as crude and childish in face of our Promethean venture, have turned around in our minds. The scientific ride, whether to outer space or into nuclear structure, has led to a dead end, a lie; uncontrollable appetite, the good life, the limitless earth, peace and plenty. Political leaders gave the lie clout, urged its huckstering. Were not we in possession of "the facts"? We know it now; they were stone cold mad. They debated soberly (the debate goes on, to this day) how many MIRVs each side must have, how best to terrorize their mad opposite numbers. One walks the streets of New York, one walks anywhere in the world, and survives only by saying to his or her soul: Anything, literally anything, can happen to me, to others, to all of us.

Revelation casts a third eye toward the blind. If the nations have gone mad, God need not do so. And it is not a law of nature that we must follow the mad pipers into the mountain. Let us start from another supposition, other ground than theirs.

The "nations," understood as the powers and pushers of this world's trashy ethos, owe God a debt. The debt is the blood of the saints. Calling in the debt, since God's other name is Mercy, is a prelude to possible conversion. Hence the church, a peaceable and peacemaking sign, stands before this mad world, and impossibly, tirelessly, calls on the world to stop being itself. But for this conversion to occur (and not the opposite) mercy must intervene, in quite merciless fashion. Not to save believers from death, prison, sweet damnation; quite the opposite — to strengthen them. For a tragic scenario is being played out. The church refuses to be eaten or embraced to death by the state. The state advances, all gab and grab, to do its usual thing. Its logic, whoever refuses to be annexed, must be punished. And since the church cannot finally be eaten or colonized (or so we believe) it must be punished. The vengeance in fact proceeds, on schedule.

But then, at a point of which we are unsure, and in a form of which we are unsure, all hell breaks loose. And it breaks loose against the state itself, which had presumed to be God; against Christians also, caught by the calamity; also, against nature, since the presumptuous paw extended there, too.

Our puzzle today, our trouble, is not the form or timing of the calamities; we have seen them all. But we do not see the struggle proceeding on these classical terms: church versus empire. Some even assert that since the church is in no trouble, and since there are states which are beyond doubt troublemakers, it must follow that there exists no church. This would seem to be true, since in the book under discussion, combat with the imperial state all but *defines* the church. (Which is by

The Nightmare of God

no means to deny that other "stances," activities, define her as well; these would include worship, intercession, truth-telling, compassion.) But we are certainly justified in asking: What becomes of the church if all other elements of her life are present, and she still finds no point of conflict with the state; nor the state with her?

Where is the church, who is she, in this culture, now? The question is a harrowing one. If our ethic is promissory, we believe the promise is faithful; therefore the church is somewhere, is some one. But if the church becomes attached to the elements of this world, then she is no longer the church, but merely an element of this world; and her fate is cut loose from those promises which properly belong to the faithful. Her fate joins that of the nations: simply the wrath of God. It is all quite brutal and simple.

This episode of Revelation (Rev. 8:2 ff) speaks of the sounding of trumpets, a flourish, the approach of an event (or series of events) of some moment. The trumpets speak. There follows a terrifying plague of disasters, hail and fire and blood. Yet disaster is not total; the limiting power of God is evident. A third of the earth is burned, a third of the trees destroyed, a third of the living creatures die, a third of the ships at sea are sunk. Whatever disasters befall, they are part of a living system, an organism of choice, response, accountability. Not all will go under, not everything come down. We think of the promise made after the flood: "Never again shall the whole world perish."

There is a large measure of death in the trumpets passage (almost as much as there is in daily life). More, an idolatry of death. Death has even become an object of worship. At the same time, in a strange network of oppositions and ironies, death is also an object of aversion and horror. How sweet the skin to its inhabitant, how precious (our skin, that is, our material well-being and health)! Deprived of these idols, life becomes unbearable. Life is the good life, why should it not go on forever? This is the idolatry John is combating. The lives of those in power, those in privilege, are so valued, so guarded (so selfish, so desirable) that death is the ultimate tragedy.

Death hovers nearby. Evicted from the technological paradise, humans are reduced today to a scramble for survival, dog eat dog. And death has no good news for the faithless.

Another story indeed for the faithful community. For them, death comes as a grace; it is all a meeting, a return, a lover's embrace. "Come, Lord Jesus." Indeed, for such, death has lost its sting.

Death is one thing; human immortality another. The difference merits our attention. Immortality in the flesh is never promised to believers, indeed, it is hardly mentioned in the Bible, except as another trap for the infidels. Believers share the common life, the common suffering; it is not to be thought wonderful that they share the common fate. We die, like all others. But with a difference: the promise, rebirth. Certainly death — in Jesus' case, in our own. But in every case, God, so to speak, does not play god. He dies, He rises again. And so will we, beyond any doubt.

Immortality, rebirth; there is, one might agree, a life and death difference. On the one hand, the Lord's promise, austere, death-embracing, life-giving. Then another sort of promise, ominous, seductive. The promise of immortality, announced today in the advanced countries, backed by a most impressive "peace-time" technology. Medicine, we are assured, will make us immortal; at least in the sense that successive victories over death and disease, extended longevity, better housing and nourishment, will indefinitely keep death at bay. Thus we will wipe death out — or at least deflect its assault. No longer are we to undergo it, get beyond it, transcend it, rise from it; we will once and for all, do away with it.

This magniloquent nonsense, it must be stressed, is strictly hometown news, a project in the hands of the "developed" peoples only. We are the immortals. We deserve to possess and dominate the world — forever. Let us then do so, with the same sublime aplomb with which we apply any other technique, whether The Bomb, or the flight to the moon; it can be done, therefore it should be done.

But there is another, darker side to this reasoning. According to the logic of our fantasies, we are slowly edging death off the scene. We are in fact multiplying death around the world. Cheap death, mass death, is the price of immunity from death. What results is, of course, a madly deranged view of both life and death, a schizoid situation. Immortality is the dream, for ourselves, multiplied death is the reality for others. Can we in fact work both wonders?

Revelation offers a different, more austere field of choice. Either one undergoes death, and thus transcends death; or one avoids it, dreads it, puts it off, and in plain fact, proceeds, to inflict it on others. The price of technological immortality — heart transplants, expensive and rare drugs, lobotomies, "cosmetic" surgery — is the death of others, always. The two together, inevitably. The price of Western, white Christian or post-Christian immortality is death for the world, multiplied; the reward is also the avenger. Internally as well, as in the world at large, one might add.

This is the judgment of Revelation; the appetite for immortality is the fruit of hatred of life.

This may be news to us; it is no news across the world. The poor, the wretched and exploited, learn from infancy that the earth belongs to Americans; that American resources, money, research, goods and services, are in bondage to death; to the arms race, sale of arms, research for better and more lethal arms. In this mad scene, allocation of brains and research is given over to death. The service of life is strictly extracurricular. And one must add that just as such a mentality and value system begins at home, so it finally comes home. Here, too, people die needlessly of neglect, children starve, the cities are a vast human waste. Death is the head of this house.

Revelation penetrates all this, in a majestic panoply of images, one nightmare melding with another, one reinforcing another. Death is at once cosmic, personal, psychological; it is also racist, sexist, competitive, power-hungry, demonic. In the cosmos as in the person, it pretends to be in the saddle, to run things, to have the final say. None of this is true; yet scripture never attempts to deny a certain empery — death cannot be evaded. Rather, it is to be confronted, undergone, and finally transcended. Paul dares to say, "I die every day." He also says, "If we have died in Christ, we shall also rise with Him."

This appetite, this grasping at immortality, obsessed and deluded as it is, leads with horrid finality to the superstate and its super wars. The point is too obvious to require further dwelling on. But it should be clear after the history of two world wars, pogroms, mass extermination, and the conduct of the crowned cannibal emperors and colonels, that the horseman named Death, once set loose in the world, takes his revenge also on his trainers and owners. He always hankers after his native pasture; and he is still named Death.

Inevitably, the longing for immortality also attaches itself to the cycles of nature, to a subhuman organic world with no transcendent implication, no tribute paid to the giver of life. Such cyclic immortality is entirely earthborne, dependent on the values and energies of the world. There it dwells, without anchor or bond, deprived of compassion, the drive of hope unachieved, the dense and tragic human scene, sacrifice.

Here and now, in the midst of universal degradation of life, immortality is dangled before the spoiled children for a price. One can live forever in a parking lot next to a Safeway. One may eat lettuce and grapes, harvested by the exploited and degraded poor. The air is foul, housing deteriorates, prices are up, wars go on and on. And people are madly in love with such a "retirement plan." They want it to go on forever — to go on going down, forever. Immortality! A sour fruit indeed, a rotten lotus. It ignores the realities the Bible opens up; the tragic character of human life, of which death is part and substance and termination — very nearly the last word, in fact, nearly the last gasp.

The reference to the star named "wormwood" is also of moment. "A huge star blazing like a torch dropped from the sky and fell on a third of the rivers and fresh water springs." (Rev. 8:10) Water pollution in the Bible! "A third of the water turned to wormwood, and people in large numbers died of the water because it was poisoned." Wormwood, symbol of the idolatrous community, the nation of pseudo faith and factual infidelity, poisons the streams of life. Here, outer and inner destruction go forward, hand in glove; right ecology or wrong, it all begins in the soul.

Through ecological awareness, one becomes spiritually observant of a moral order in body, soul, life and community. Such a sense of things reaches out, embracing the very grasses of the field, the waters of the streams, the commonest and humblest elements of creation. But if I pollute, it is because I am polluted. If I spread disorder and garbage about, it is because my soul is a dumping ground. Thus Revelation, a profound consonance between spiritual and material realities.

> *When he unlocked the shaft of the abyss, smoke poured out of the*

> *abyss like the smoke from a huge furnace so that the sun and the sky were darkened by it.* (Rev. 9:2)

The blowing of the fifth trumpet brings more pollution. The abyss is an ancient symbol, signifying the collective bad conscience, the chaos of wrong choice, selfishness, personal and social disarray. From these things arise the revenge of nature against criminal men, the furies, the revulsion of violated nature. Self-hatred spills over into hatred of the universe, threatens to bring all things to an end.

In the same vein, mysterious locusts with human faces invade the landscape. The plagues of Egypt come to mind, but with a difference: John gives the avengers a nightmarish phiz. The locusts, a devouring plague in fact wear our own faces. Is the face of evil other than human? One recalls the photos of American helicopters darkening the sky over Vietnam. Seeing those aerial horrors, I thought of this passage: locusts with human faces. A cloud of engines of destruction over the landscape, a sound of myriad gigantic locusts, an iron, technological buzz that fell on the ear like the approach of doom. Is this how the shadow of America hovers over the world?

A series of plagues follows the trumpet blasts, parallel to the catastrophes following the unsealing of scrolls. The imperial dream is broken. It had aimed the gun sights of its internal violence elsewhere; abroad, far from its own cities. Other peoples and landscapes are forever expendable. But we, and our playground, never. Alas, the Bible suggests in a hundred ways that such a dream is ill-founded. In these matters, every wind is a prevailing one; every form of technical ruin seeded elsewhere, comes home. Every secret decision to destroy or subjugate others becomes at some point brutally, publicly domesticated. Every strike against the earth strikes back at the aggressor. (Rm. 8:21; Mt. 24:28)

Ignatius Loyola had a vision of the powers and spirits of earth, rising against the sinner to take their vengeance. In Luke's gospel, the psychological details of the day of wrath are stressed; he speaks of the "distress of nations ... perplexity ... people fainting with fear and foreboding." (Lk. 21:25-26)

When a culture is crumbling, degradation of conscience comes first. One accepts, "lives with" ever greater public violence; in consequence, one yields to new depths of despair, dread, ennui, moral nausea. Finally, the horror is simply shrugged off; it is not one's affair, let the whole thing go to hell.

> *When this happens, people will long for death and will not find it anywhere; they will want to die, and death will evade them.* (Rev. 9:6)

The search after death goes on, in the midst of the rake's progress, the dealing of death. Men and women seek death out — first and foremost as the evil servant of their hatred and fear. Hidden from them is an insupportable irony: They want simply to die. In this way, the meaning of war, well camouflaged, like a nuclear bunker under a green cover, erupts as an urge toward social suicide. The death urge is universalized, idolized. And finally it becomes a criminal act to seek life, to resist death.

In John's vision, death edges closer. People stretch out their arms to embrace what they have so long inflicted on others. And ironically, death plays a hideous charade, a lover's game. It evades them. They utterly despised life, they murdered others. Now, they seek death, but they cannot touch their demon lover. The dance of death wheels on, a mirage, a cruel charade, just out of reach. (This is a form of despair, a game, let it be pointed out, that flourishes on both sides of the social barricades, left and right.)

> [The locusts] *were told to attack only those who were without God's seal on their foreheads.* (Rev. 9:4)

Believers are to be protected. One might ask realistically: How? If the community is resisting death, it would follow that its members stand in the forefront of suffering; they take the blows first and longest. Then how this claim? Surely we are not to conjure up some magical compound within which the initiates cower, chanting sutras while the skies come down....

The promise seems to be two-edged. The faithful endure everything, including death; but they will live once more. Moreover, in the midst of struggle, they are gifted with miraculous long sufferance, precisely because they are literate, because they know the promise, believe, have access to a truth which lies beyond the so-called "facts."

The number "seven" flowers into another seven. That number is important, a symbol of perfection. The first septenary, the unsealing of the scrolls, set loose calamities of human willfulness: wars, famines, invasions and death. Now the trumpets sound a blast of natural disasters. The ecology of the world is ruined, consequent upon moral evil. This is the view of Revelation, in consonance with Genesis itself. The world is blasted in its natural beauties, spent in its resources; its fecundity, as a result of human evil. Evil spills over into the universe, blights everything. Or, from another point of view, the natural universe is ruined. Not because of storms, cyclones, droughts, quakes (in which a process of recovery and mutuality is always going on), but in the biblical view, moral evil ricochets off, wounds, blights the world of nature.

Teaching vividly the mutuality and interplay of all beings, Revelation naturally invites comparison with Genesis. In that account, the corporate nature of the universe, in its beginning and its "fall," is simply taken for granted. And that cosmic web is explored again in Revelation — for good and ill. No one is saved in isolation, no part of the universe is destroyed apart from any other; evil in the moral order results in the destruction of the universe. This sense of things enlarges on the earlier vision. The fall of man and woman was the fall of creation; their choice had enormous reverberations in the natural world. Paul's letter to the Romans celebrates the same themes; creation groans for rebirth, under the heel of a mysterious misfortune. Further, he declares: As in Adam all fell, so in Christ all are reborn.

Whenever that is, an event of spiritual import occurs, it vibrates in mysterious measure, not only in each member of the human family, but in the natural world as well.

This is the integrity of the biblical world view. It is simply unimaginable that one stand alone in the universe, without roots, tentacles, moral vibrations outward; and similarly, no one gets reborn alone. All such events interact, as our present age is seeing, to its immense discomfiture. And sin, properly and biblically understood, cannot be regarded or judged solely on a one-to-one basis. One-to-one is all-to-all. The sins of corporations are corporate sins, a revealing tautology. Moral evil, property-idolatry, threaten the world's well-being. The Bomb is by no means a chancy event. It was brought to pass by us — but prior to that horror, it exploded within us.

Finally, the web of evil is broken. Finally, a figure of hope emerges; an angel described in terms of utmost dignity: descending from heaven, robed in cloud, a rainbow around his head, his face like the sun, his legs like pillars of fire. (Rev. 10:1-7) The symbols are charged with meaning. The cloud and pillar of fire are signs of divine presence and protection; the rainbow: a sign of hope, promise, covenant. John brings them all together. The angel is quite simply the symbol of God's abiding and faithful presence with the community.

He has an announcement. He holds a little scroll open in his hand, sets his right foot on the sea and his left on land.

> *The angel I saw standing on sea and land raised his right hand to heaven and swore by him who lives forever, who created heaven, earth and sea and everything in them, "There shall be no more delay. When the time comes for the seventh angel to blow his trumpet, the sacred purpose of God will have been accomplished."* (Rev. 10:5-7)

This angel is an epiphany of the spirit of God, in the midst of land and sea and heavens. How concrete, how earthy the image! Everything in creation is drawn into the vision, as though this figure were weaving together, healing, uniting the universe. After the horror announced by the trumpets, comes the angel of ecology, the spirit of the restored world. And he swears not by some transcendent remote God, but by God the creator. A sacred and beautiful implication; God is known through the beauty of the world. So, His angel swears by the one who created heaven, earth, sea, everything in them, a sign of restoration, of peace after conflict, of friendship healed.

"There shall be no more delay." People are in deepest trouble. The angel comes to reassure, to restore the covenant; to remind us that earthly events, though

The Nightmare of God 55

tragic and death-ridden, are still in the hands of providence. This is a message to the community of faith, to set hope stirring in a hopeless time. The purpose of God is accomplished; the healing and resurrection of the universe and the human community are underway; renewal, rebirth, ecological and moral integrity, the diffusion of love. And repose, in spite of all!

The "great oath" of the angel is a reassurance also to the church. In order to endure travail, one must have a sense of victory. Such a sense gives credibility to the struggle.

Meantime (all time is mean time) the struggle has its own validity, in light of the promise. Through it we keep on the qui vive for the breakthrough; despite all, we even become worthy of sharing it.

The angel spans with his breadth of wisdom and love, all creation, the works of God by whom he swears. The scene is one of immense power and beauty. So dramatic a moment is of great import to the faithful. Is it enough to say: We have the covenant, we have the example of Christ ... what more is needed? What is needed is, after all, what is granted: a renewal of vows at a time of crisis, terror, demoralization. New strength is granted the initial resolve.

To be noted also, is that the angelic oath favors only those who are in combat with the forces of death.

The Eating of the Little Scroll

> *Then I heard the voice I had heard from heaven speaking to me again. "Go," it said, "and take that open scroll out of the hand of the angel standing on sea and land." I went to the angel and asked him to give me the small scroll, and he said, "Take it and eat it; it will turn your stomach sour, but in your mouth it will taste as sweet as honey." So I took it out of the angel's hand, and swallowed it; it was as sweet as honey in my mouth, but when I had eaten it my stomach turned sour. Then I was told, "You are to prophesy again, this time about many different nations and countries and languages and emperors."*
> (Rev. 10:8 ff)

Swallow the truth, whole and entire. The eating of the scroll suggests a contrast with the mere tasting, sipping of Christian life; a dilettante's distraction; or a cafeteria-style picking and choosing among delicacies of doctrine.

The Bible has many such episodes, humiliating personal gestures exacted of the prophet. These are commonly sources of new realization, as well as dramatic warnings, hearkenings, moments of truth. Thus Jeremiah is instructed to put on a yoke like a beast and walk abroad. The people are to know that slavery awaits them. Again he is told to break a clay jar and hold the shards aloft; Israel too will be broken.

The signs require thought. The prophet, in obedience to the God of signs, is plucked from ordinary activity; from that "round" of money, lust, power, and plain unconsciousness which allow the cycle of death to spin on and on. Stepping aside from all this does make of the prophet a "special case"; he remains quotidian, plodding, humble, accessible to others. In order to speak for God, he must "comedown, comedown."

Earlier in Revelation Jesus was given power to unseal the scroll; now John is told to eat the scroll. The question arises, why did Jesus not eat the large scroll? Because in the deepest sense He has already done so; history has passed through His guts. So He has power over the contents; He sets its forces in motion. But John has yet to absorb the truth, to get it inside him. Thus for him, eating becomes a symbol for the intussesception of truth. In a parallel way, Jesus says, "Eat my flesh and drink my blood." That is, get the truth flowing through you. Absorb it into your vitals. You cannot arrive at the truth by looking at it, by smelling it, by hearing it; you must consume it.

The angel adds mysteriously, "It will be sweet in your mouth and bitter in your guts." Is this because the gospel seems easy to absorb in the beginning, and only afterward becomes a bitter travail? In any case, a good description of the truth. We eat to our peril; salvation is dangerous business.

Idols: i.e., Whatever Turns You On

> *But the rest of the human race, who escaped these plagues, refused either to abandon the things they had made with their own hands — the idols made of gold, bronze, stone and wood that can neither see nor hear nor move — or to stop worshipping devils. Nor did they give up their murdering, or witchcraft, or fornication or stealing.* (Rev. 9:20-21)

There is no more sorrowful, recurrent motif in Revelation than this: The nations are stuck in a moral impasse. The wicked emerge from catastrophe, to grasp their idols once more. The outcome of suffering is murderously ambiguous. All suffer; a few are strengthened, the majority are worsened. The Bible knows us, uncomfortably well!

The text suggests a new division; no more winners and losers, but a universal loss, everything coming down, indiscriminate ruin. And within this devastation, a remnant survives, identifiable, believers after the event, as they were before it.... Others, also identifiable, after the fact as before, clutch their idols, in the endless hot pursuit of death.

Idolatry yields its ground literally before no event, no visitation, when the idol is so far-reaching, so deeply embedded, so intransigently proud, as the nation super state (or super church) and its deluded members. There is a closely gauged connection here between the search for death and the persistence of idolatry. We do not go empty-handed on that search; we go, idols in hand. And what idol is grasped most tenaciously of all? The idol of death. The very search for death is idolatry, the fullest possible tribute to the powers of the world, the explicit denial of resurrection; therefore, the denial of Christ.

The Bible is considerably more somber, realistic than most of us would allow. Disaster does not ordinarily change people, except for the worse. As they were, so they remain. If they believe, they may indeed be purified; but if they serve idols, disaster changes nothing; they continue to serve with greater enthusiasm. So the passage is a wicked parody of the search for God entered on by the just. These seek and find Him; the others seek out their god, death; and he eludes them. The faithless long to consummate their service by the ultimate adoration, which is to say, self-extinction. But they cannot summon the genie who says, do it! Their will is not sufficiently strong, even in diabolism, to conjure up the devil. The form in which they seek him is not the one he has assumed. He would prefer to ape the god of life. (Rev. 13)

A link between death-seekers and idolaters is forged here; it invites meditation. From the world's side, the news about human achievement is invariably Promethean. Limitless possibility, an ever-receding frontier; it opens up as we advance; an elusive world, enough for all (translated, "for us"). The scientific method encourages this folly. And if the earth should by some mischance begin to fail (even to fail us), to lose its reserves, we invoke the demon of the atom from the bottle, the savior, the renewer, the inexhaustible servant, genie, source.

This braggadocio is broken by the truth. We are not gods at all; we are in no way even godlike, except as we ape our own gods; in craven fear of death, overweening pride, the passion to kill and dominate and "prove" ourselves. These themes, the "one third" passages suggest quite powerfully. The earth has a limit, the human has a limit. To overpass a creaturely measure is not to surpass ourselves; it is to invoke the demons of unreality; and with regard to the earth, to bring on a sure revenge. For if we refuse to live in a certain creaturely peace with the earth, it will make war on us, by so simple a tactic as cutting the umbilical that joins our fate to its own. And if that line of life is cut, we die, before birth, before rebirth. Thus, if "one third" is destroyed, whether of the natural world or of world population, a clear total is indicated; as well as a limit. Gargantua, Prometheus, Colossus; his measure is taken.

The images of humankind offered here are degraded, diminished, anti-human. But who would say they are untruthful, that they deny the truth of our woe?

Catastrophe leads to no moral change. Misfortune, biblically, is sometimes a sign of God's disapproval; it is designed to lead people to repentance, to change idolatrous lives. Here the plan gets nowhere. The Bible admits it — God is defeated. "Those who survived these plagues did not abjure the gods their hands had fashioned, nor cease their worship of false gods, nor repent of their crimes." One theory of popular religion would have it that an earthquake, fire, flood causes people to become more thoughtful; they take stock of themselves, they change. The Bible is more realistic; maybe rebirth — but also maybe not!

In this instance, this nightmare, the exact opposite of conversion occurs. Misfortune crushes people's moral sense, they continue in a worse state than before. This theme will be repeated throughout the Revelation, an extremely sobering view of human life.

Idolatry is the issue. It goes to the heart of the biblical message. Two scornful phrases about idols are invoked constantly in the Old Testament. They are "work of men's hands," images that "cannot see, cannot talk or hear." Certainly not the true God, because fashioned by human hands. Mute and blind and halt and dumb; whereas God sees and speaks, hears and responds.

More. Bad worship is strangely connected here with public crime. One cannot justly express the connections by explaining that people go into a corner, worship a piece of wood and, in consequence, kill their brothers and sisters. This is a caricature of the biblical idea. But suppose a person hates his brother and (perhaps only in his heart) murders him. Such hatred already makes such a one an idolater. The connection is a close one; hatred of life is a consequence of false worship. The idol symbolizes a force, a concentrated energy of death in the heart. People worship their hatred of life, pride, lust, love of money. The final idol is one's own disordered soul; one hearkens to it, obeys it, follows its appetites, a very god.

Such self-worship is also dramatized in public crime. The criminality may go under many names, in many bloody directions — hatred of God, hatred of another, thirst for conflict, hateful divisions, feverish envy, unrest of spirit. In denouncing such idolatries, the Bible is by no means scoring a primitive urge that modern men and women have triumphantly outgrown. Rather the biblical symbols suggest how people choose to live, at any point of time. The Bible is not condemning primitive Indians or Polynesians or Africans. Revelation, if it means anything, is excoriating nuclear savages, post-Christians. Just as Revelation drew on the history of Babylon to point out the spiritual condition of Rome, so believers today are invited to consider their own lives, times, political climate, myths, symbols.

The question inevitably arises once more: What do men and women worship today? Perhaps through Revelation we may touch the pith of things, our illusions clarified, our obsessions laid out, our fears and hatreds placed before us. It may become clear in consequence that the works of our hands are idols also — whether technology, propaganda, politics, the family, the race, the thirst to win, to justify this or that ideology.

The idols cannot see or hear or speak; they are ultimately, the Bible says, mere objects, artifacts of gold, silver, bronze, stone, and wood. Today, primitive ikons and statues have been fused anew — into artifacts both subtle and complex, whether machinery for the moon or machinery for a bomber. They exert the same quasi-religious tug on the heart. And they lead nowhere.

What does the Bible mean by accusing us of worshipping those things? Surely no one kneels in front of a nuclear silo. Or does one? No one kneels before a Phantom Jet. No one kneels before a dollar.... The truth is otherwise. We perform such quasi-religious acts continually, a favorite pastime. We kneel, we give our heart to, give our life to, run after, sacrifice all for, this or that weapon, this image of ourselves, that beckoning idol, whenever the life and dignity of others are declared expendable to our indifference, envy, cupidity, violence.

Finally, idolatry is a radical deflection of life's energies into human destruction. Those energies are meant to flow clear, pure, uninterrupted in the direction of God and others, in service and love. But idolatry muddles, befouls, pollutes our hearts in the service of death. Goods and services are neglected, research goes where the money goes: into more and more subtle, skillful, anti-human, indiscriminate instruments of death.

Another application of the idol image must include the media, the so-called "facts" (more often a barrage of propaganda and special pleading — awakening an itch for possessions and superfluities). The facts more often than not so rigged, plucked from context, cosmeticized, vandalized, as to become merely factitious; they literally make no sense. The facts are concocted "by human hands," in the sense that they pander to appetite, curiosity, distraction.

Such objects, images, arouse in us a kind of worship; they demand attention, they color experience, they throw us off balance, excite our cupidity, awaken pride of place, fuel our envy and hatreds. But they cannot see, cannot help us, cannot go anywhere, contain no wisdom, do not lead beyond themselves. They are free-floating, inert; they awaken no compassion, awaken only despair.

When facts become an end in themselves, rather than means to wisdom, people become media freaks, idolators, eye consumers. Their idol is simply the media. But the medium is dead; there is no message. The tube pours out an unassimilable barrage, inert knowledge — instead of helping us unify a moral view of the world, it scrambles our heads. After a time, people become like dead tubes gazing at tubes.

Such facts awaken no interest in a compassionate, serviceable view of the world. One thinks of the claims made during the Vietnam War, of the impact of media in conveying the bloody truth, arousing consciences. If such was the virtue of media, should not one day of such a war have been enough, surely one day offered a generous quota of deaths? Yet the war went on for some fifteen years; all the while Americans were bombarded with the "facts" of the war. Indeed, the war became a war game, played out grotesquely in cozy, safe surroundings. The living room became a war room; room, so to speak, for more and more death. And all during those years, media apologists were marveling — have we ever known the truth so shockingly? Is this not the first war in which our people have had "the facts"? Alas, it went on forever, our longest war (and most savage).

And the lying claims continue. Bombarded by the "facts of life," people cannot arrive at appropriate action or moral unity. Either they see no place for themselves in the world and give up in despair, or they join that world, its lockstepping legions of "good citizens."

The war went on; the legions lurked and fought and died in our living rooms. Was the war thereby more civilized? Was a future war rendered less likely? One is allowed to be sceptical. Indeed, a kind of balance is needed for sanity's sake today; one must allow for a certain freedom from the facts, space apart from the facts. One must in fact create a kind of contemplative attitude in face of the media frenzy. Otherwise we go insane.

In sum, Revelation illustrates the queasy relationship between bad times and moral change — a connection about which the Bible is generally sceptical, if not downright pessimistic. Then, the texts draw attention to idolatry, specifically to the likeness it bears (even in the root of the word) with ideology. Idolatry and Ideology — formulas, pseudo-realities people live by, which, in most cases, keep them from the truth of life. And, thirdly, a connection is suggested between idolatry and crime. This sorry truth comes home most surely in our lifetime, in the reality of war — the organized violence of states. That is to say, if our hearts are given over to instruments of destruction, we will surely put these idols to service; idolatry will create crime. And in that process, our conscience will be so altered that we will accept more and more death, as a hellish fact of life. Our level of tolerance will rise and rise; as indeed it did during the Vietnam years. (No war in history brought the "acceptable" — powerful word! — "level" of civilian death to so bloody a pitch.) An idolatry of weaponry and power led to crime, which in turn led to a change in consciousness; such a blunting of moral sense that toward the end of the war, it was difficult to find in most Americans a moral turn-off point. One could put the question: At what level of war crime would you say no? One could discover no such level; none existed. And this was true, though prior to the war such people had rather clear ideas on the moral limits of violence, would not have allowed or remained silent before crimes which, a few years later, they were tranquilly bearing. Public violence marched on our souls and possessed us. It was as simple as that.

Revelation, unlike many of the Old Testament documents, does not speak of the idols as "dead images." The psalms and prophets deride the devotees of idols, which "have tongues and speak not, ears and hear not." This is not John's view of the idols; his is rather secular and social. The idols are human institutions, possessed; therefore possessive, reaching out, grasping. Theirs is a tremendous volatile energy, an energy of violence, chaos and cunning. Ultimately, they press a religious claim, they demand both awe and worship.

They press their cause with a kind of hideous metaphysical necessity: You are mine. Money-making, ego-stroking, conferring and withholding honors, the idols are summed up in the state, its institutions, tools, skills, control and coercion; instructing, purveying, transforming, degrading.

We note also the "secularization" and "sacralization" of the idols in current culture. On the one hand, there is no vital paganism worth talking about, in the sense of which the "seven letters to the churches" speak; there are no longer adversaries of this kind. Today the "idols" are transformed into the gods of secular power and authority and their institutions and consequences: war.

In another sense, today's idols are totally religious. How else explain the spirit that blesses secular idols, in effect granting them godly space and character? Further, how explain a Christianity which embraces this world of darkness, is silent before war and war preparation, assures warring nations that God is on this side and that, a schizoid god, a christened Mars? This is a diabolic ecumenism, a sacral idolatry.

We must also grant in the light of Revelation, that these idols, powers, dominations, have an existence separate from our own. They are not merely extrapolated egos, so to speak (though their consonance with our nightmarish pride and selfishness is one aspect of their enticement, a bargain struck in the dark). Essentially, as Revelation indicates, the demons are maleficent spirits who imbed themselves in human life and institutions, and from there proceed to turn history around, in a direction neither pro-human nor godlike.

Their activity is suggested in Revelation — they blind us to our true situation, our bandage to the power of death. So death grows more commonplace; it is even purveyed as an instrument of social change.

- They "normalize" the abnormal; especially in areas of acceptable violence. Yesterday's horror becomes today's stereotype. "We can live with it," we say; which being translated means: We are dying of it.
- They deride and reject promissory conduct. Faithlessness becomes the rule — if not of faith, then of thumb.
- They experiment with and extend the metaphors of death, in every direction: social, personal, psychological. Thus the rule of death becomes the rule of the imagination as well. After a given time, we cannot so much as imagine any alternative human arrangement than the one we are enslaved to — whether educational, legal, medical, political, religious, familial. The social contract narrows, the socialization becomes a simple brainwash. Alternative ways, methods, styles are ignored, or never created.
- They politicize, economize, propagandize, all (formerly) moral questions, taking them from the empery of Christ's return and emptying them of their promissory character; that is to say, of mystery.
- They make life and death and everything between the subject of merely political competence.

A further question is implied in Revelation. If the Bible warns of a drift toward the acceptance of death as a social method, how does one declare a limit to that acceptance? If moral life is generally adrift, and one wishes not to drift, what does one seize upon, in order to stop drifting? Is there a foothold or a handhold? It must be admitted that for most Americans there simply is none. The quality of life has gone down and down; the point is not that city streets are filthy, or even that the air is a pool of bad cess. Something other than this; people in fact expect less of themselves and of one another; live with more violence, more noise, more crowding, more friction.

I remember returning to New York after some time in prison. Then came the shock. The first cab I stepped into was exactly like a federal marshal's car, the only difference being, I had no handcuffs on. Still, as far everything else was concerned, I was back in a barricaded paddywagon. Remote control in the front locked the rear doors, a bulletproof shield stood between passenger and driver; one could scarcely talk to him, he could hardly hear. You put your money in a little slot, he took it on the other side. An extraordinary conveyance! When the passenger was ready to get out, the driver pulled a button, the rear doors unlocked, you were released. Thousands of cabs are outfitted that way now. Expectation; symbols about life, about violence.

If this is the drift of things, two questions arise. First, can we even recognize the drift, being immersed in it? Then, is a countercurrent possible? And if so, how does one get it underway? How does one live today a life that is recognizably human?

Social structures normally produce people ready to join the drift, with few resources to question where the drift is leading, or why one should not join it, or how not to join it, or where to go, presuming one does not want to join it. It must be said that most structures merely channel people into that drift — in many cases in order to speed it up.

Only a small minority retain a sense of themselves, as they embark on adult life; such a sense as endows them with wisdom and compassion of soul — the capacity to create a countercurrent.

In Western culture today, we discover such gifts almost solely among the despised of the earth, people whom the drift itself has cast aside — minorities, women, poor people. This is of course a biblical idea; one is not dreaming up something sentimental in so speaking. In God's view, history is carried along, its burdens, its hope, by those whom the Bible calls the "anawim," the wretched of the earth. Out of the matrix of their culture rises this ability to survive the awesome grinder of competition and public violence. They come upon the clues necessary to live differently, to live without killing, degrading, imprisoning, torturing. Where death flourishes among the majority, life prevails among a few. Let us rejoice.

The Beast From the Sea

Then I saw a beast emerge from the sea. It had seven heads and ten horns, with a crown on each of its ten horns, and its heads were marked with blasphemous titles. (Rev. 13:1)

Who is the beast? Who is he to us?

He emerges from the sea, a descendant of the vision of Daniel; the four beasts, symbols of the four Eastern dynasties. Here, all four are gathered in one. It is a striking implication, filled with menace; a warning. Rome, in its pretension and blasphemy, sums up imperial history. No empire starts its history from scratch; each, John implies, gathers up all the arrogant wisdom, the baleful myths, the violent skills, that marked previous empires; renews, unites, goes further.

Some initial reflections:

- The beast image moves in at least two directions. It is not merely the super state, its claims, domination, armies, political savvy; it is also ourselves. It "comes from the sea"; from the depths of human conscience and consciousness.

- The beast is fat with history, with contemporary meaning. He is self-renewing, we will never have done with him. Again and again, the imperial will arises, flourishes, murders, enslaves — and vanishes. John is ultimately pointing to a cliché: The vocation of empire is to self-destruct.

- It would be bad enough, if the empire were merely seeking again and again, to dominate the world's structures. But this is an abstraction, and should leave us uneasy; especially today. The beast's mark is murder, the mark of Cain. It is also his method, first, foremost. We have but to look around us.

- Separation of empire and religion is not verified; not for long. The beast wants religion as he wants every other legitimate area of freedom and transcendence. The "inclusion" of religion thus marks the rise of empire. Except, of course, for the Pentecost people (neither "pentecostal" nor "charismatic," as commonly understood). They are the faithful or beloved community of Revelation. Their offense: They will neither eat nor be eaten.

- The trouble these troublesome folks have is not in dealing with the secular powers as such. Everyone needs streets cleaned, mails delivered, traffic lights installed. But beyond these rather pedestrian needs; above, beyond, within, the state moves. The trouble is perversion and inflation of legitimate state activity. To the point where a properly religious fealty is demanded. Kill, be killed, all in the name of the Dragon, the Beast, the Unholy Spirit. At this point, faith draws a line.

The ultimate knee-bending before the state is service in its wars. Prior to that, people have to be conditioned. In Rome, the emperors went to all sorts of absurd lengths to bend the people round; from bread and circuses for the idlers, to colossal statues for the churchgoers. But this was mere window-dressing. The real question was literally one of life and death.

> "Historians are agreed that this religious intensification of the political achievement of Rome was a stroke of genius. Through this 'religion,' a spiritual unity and compactness was given to the vast empire which, with its varied geographical and ethnological composition, it would never have otherwise attained. The brilliant figure of emperor Augustus stands at the head of this religious, visible unity of the empire, the symbol of political monotheism. This was bound to lead to sharp conflict. Christians could have coexisted under excellent terms with the Roman Empire as such. The state was a strong political power; justice and tolerance, and its worldwide political system had made the swift expansion of Christianity possible. ... Yet for all this, praise of the Roman state comes late; the church is silent on the subject until Constantine. A long trail led to that point, an acute and bloody conflict. The church was faced with a political religion, a political monotheism whose symbol was the emperor. Conflict was inevitable." (Lilje, *The Last Book of the Bible*)

■ One should take seriously the fascination created by such secular power. It corrupts not merely those who exercize it, but those who are drawn to it, accede to it, concentrate on it, grant it a substance it by no means possesses. One would like to protest; such power has no power over me. But in fact, such a protest, as a mere statement, is useless. A style is called for, a turning about. The Beast must be brought down to size, must hear us say (but mostly with our lives, unbestial): You are a liar and a murderer. You do not stand outside the law, you do not stand within Christianity. You are not a god. More to the point, you are in no sense human. But words here are nearly worthless. We are in another realm entirely, that of civil disobedience.

■ There is no "successful" resistance, in a worldly sense. There is only "defeat." The word is John's; one is tempted to add, he should know. Indeed, the word "success" is no more than a sop for the worldly.

■ "Captivity for those who are destined for captivity; the sword for those who are to die by the sword. This is why the saints must have constancy and faith." (Rev. 13:10) This is the climax of the chapter under discussion; the decree of God is hard as hell. Sometimes there is nothing to be done. Or rather, the only thing to be done is the finally unacceptable thing, which is to die.... The reference is clearly to Jeremiah:

> *The Lord said to me: even if Moses and Samuel stood before me, my heart would not turn toward this people. Send them away from me. If they ask you where they should go, tell them; whoever is marked for death, to death; whoever ... for the sword, to the sword; whoever ... for famine, to famine; whoever for captivity ... to captivity.* (Jr. 15:1-2)

Chapter 13 is certainly one of the most renowned episodes of Revelation; and rightly so. It is also one of the most abused, ignored, feared, misunderstood. Understandably so.

In any case, the outlines are not complicated. A kind of trinity of beasts appears. The first, a dragon figure; the second, from the sea; then a mysterious third. The first is a father image; the second, an ape of the holy Son; and the third, strangely wired to give forth sounds, speech, a kind of unholy spirit. Thus the vision of the diabolic at work, an image of the state, its panoply of power, and also, its hold on humans. In their regard the claims of the state can only be called total. And just short of ultimately successful.

"The dragon conferred upon it [the beast from the sea] his own power and rule and great authority." (Rev. 13:4) A father figure confers on another beast its authority. Out of the Old Testament arises this tremendous primordial imagery. We read in the Psalms: "This day have I begotten thee" — the Father speaking to the Son. In the vision of Ezekiel also, and in the Book of Daniel, God confers upon the Son of Man His own power. Now the secular beast apes the earlier visions. He creates his own history, his anti-Bible.

The beast is described in some detail. "It had ten horns and seven heads, on its horns were ten diadems, on each head a blasphemous name. The beast I saw was like a leopard, its feet like a bear and its mouth like a lion's mouth...." (Rev. 13:1-2) Every detail would be significant to the early Christian community. The numbers refer to titles of the Emperor; the diadems, to successive crowns, as the imperial state added to itself tribes, by conquest and treaty. And the blasphemous names are of great import: The community is confronting a promethean claim of the beast — to usurp the name of God.

The beast is a horrid nightmarish composite of ferocity and seduction — leopard, bear, lion, horned animal. The leopard, we are told, is a symbol of Persia; the bear, of Medea; the lion, of Babylon; and the ten horns, of Macedon. Everything coalesces around an image of Rome; John is obviously speaking of his own situation and that of his community. So he sums up all past imperial adventures; a composite beast comes forward; the worst instincts and characteristics of all history coalesce in Rome. Rome sums up the lethal imperial adventure, then shouts: I shall go further!

A kind of patchwork animal is invoked; it never existed on land or sea; only in nightmares. The beast thus is an apt and acute historical symbol for Rome, for the place she occupies in the history of imperial nations. A literally impossible beast! Rome had gone further along the imperial road than any previous nation. This empire was not content with conquest and domination. Her emperors went on to claim what only God may claim: divinity. No other nation had done that. The Roman empire was thus an unprecedented assault on the true God; a source of inevitable conflict therefore with the new community, a dilemma lowering its horns before the horrified gaze of believers.

The beast is crowned with ten diadems, each crown signifying a blasphemous name of God. On the coins of the realm, the emperors stamped a word *divinis or divus*, "the divine one," "the holy one." It was a title of God. They also decreed divine honors immediately after death; one of them — Nero — went so far as to demand those honors while living. Where the Greek language was in vogue (as it was in many of the eastern provinces) the coins with the head of the emperor were marked "theos," the Holy One, the God. Some borrowed the names of gods to express their divinity; Nero declared he was another Apollo, Helios, the sun god.

This creature arises from the land. His scene of conquest is already formed, from human structures, historical arrangements, a civilization. He is a figure of continuity, rather than of original creation. Someone must have gone before him — someone "out of which," the dragon arising straight out of chaos. This creature, we are told, stands for the emperor, a figure who presupposes a long political tradition.

The first figure sets things up, gets a certain human arrangement under way. The second one is an image of formed culture.

The beast has a perennial life. In verse 3: "One of his heads appeared to have received a death blow, but the mortal wound was healed...." Like a nightmare, the sentence is totally unexplained. Who healed the wound? How? Who dealt the death blow? Why? Everything is arbitrary — it is just there. The symbol hints at a kind of anti-resurrection; the beast is aping the greatest of Christ's wonders.

The text implies that the beast cannot be finally slain within time. We were led to believe, we would like to believe, that human bestiality, political bestiality, was disposed of long ago. Are we not an improvement on those who went before? Are not our political structures humane, compassionate, just? Alas, the beast is perennial, bound to the world cycle — part of the turn and turnabout of history. His power is breathtaking — he never quite dies. He cannot get reborn, but he can be healed; something quite different, but in the diabolic bestiary, quite adequate. Again and again he is patched up. He still lurches about the world — "slouches toward Bethlehem to be born." (From "The Second Coming," by W. B. Yeats) The powerful image is of the millennium, an icy secular promise, forever renewed. But what the beast cannot promise or confer — on himself or others — is new life, rebirth, moral change. He is always the beast, always the same, reappearing armed with new slogans, new credentials, new plausibility.

The beast is also enormously enticing, in his contemporary epiphany. It is always much more difficult to pierce his disguise today than to judge him as he appeared centuries ago. What enables a person or a community to cut through those tremendous, self-justifying claims, those impeccable credentials — and to utter the great refusal? According to John, very few resist the Beast. The price is too heavy, the claims unanswerable. The polluted image of the pseudo-divine is very old on the earth; he debases a divine claim by seizing it, drawing it to himself. The claim moreover does not exist in a vacuum of time and place, but takes shrewd advantage of the political atmosphere, here and now. The Beast stands with its four paws firmly on the earth; better, on the lives of people; on them his political, quasi-religious weight lies like a millstone. And the people turn to him. Like a news report shot round the world by satellite, the word races, shocking, fascistic, fantastic; and given political developments today, utterly plausible; "...the whole world went after the beast in wondering admiration ... worshipped him...." (Rev. 13:3,8)

They worshipped him first of all because the dragon had given his power over to the beast. The dragon is a father figure, a Jupiter, whose image is everywhere supreme. But his supremacy is uncertain. He is always breaking up, breaking apart, handing over specific powers to other gods. Jove is divided up, a Roman pantheon. In a stroke of divine ingenuity, he creates intermediaries, closer to the people, gods of this event, of that profession, this or that sector or special interest. Why then do they worship the bestial "son"? Because he looks like their gods, too. Their chant is weirdly logical. "Who is like the beast, who can fight against it?" (Rev. 13:4) He offers security — the security of cold despair. They might be chanting: "We've been pushed against the wall; now at least we're somewhere. We know we can go no further. But at least we need not stand in the dark, or be alone, or chart our own way — even to destruction."

In a time of upheaval, people are desperate for somewhere to stand — someone to adore — someone to tell them what is to be done. Out of the thousand and one voices, we long to hear one shouting louder than all the rest; someone who puts things together for us, so that we need not look to one another, accept obscurity, perplexity, work our own way through the darkness: Oh, God, give us a leader, give us a beast!

Today the appeal is especially powerful, one can now exalt in a mingling of religion and nationalism: Our country, right or wrong.

One cannot but contrast this with the style of Jesus: informal, human, tentative, loving, modest. Far from seeking honor, He fled it. They came en masse to make Him king. But He discerns the truth; they do not want a messiah, they want a beast. So He set sail and fled across the lake. At another time, He fled into the desert. In such circumstances there is but one thing to do, lest one be reduced to a bestial ikon: flee. The tactic of Jesus, flowing from His soul, and the tactic of the beast are thus quite different.

So, beyond doubt, is the conduct of the people who encounter each. Jesus mistrusted crowds, mass scenes, appeals that induce hysteric fealty. When the people were hungry — He fed them; then, we are told, He dismissed them. He knew that the beast hungers after crowds, fuels their volatile mood, cannot exist without their worship. He is devoured by ego; he must have this world for his own.

> The beast was allowed to mouth bombast and blasphemy and given the right to reign for forty-two months. It opened its mouth in blasphemy against God, reviling His name and His heavenly dwelling. It was also allowed to wage war on God's people and defeat them, and granted authority over every tribe and people, language and nation. All on earth will worship it, except those names the Lamb who was slain keeps in his rolls of the living, written there since the world was made. (Rev. 13:5-8)

How does the beast win a religious response if it blasphemes God? The implicit irony is clear. The bestial method is exactly apt to win such a tribute. The tactic, so to speak, works; the beast is efficient, he "makes sense." He teaches, Blaspheme God and win a following; live the Gospel and win something else.

We might be tempted to say: John is referring to an extreme case, the Roman instance. Too easy! If we live in the beast's skin (time or place are immaterial) we adopt his ways; we ape him as he apes God. John is implying that the beast recurrently, invariably, wins a following under successive political and religious guises. He does this by blaspheming the true God. One is not to imagine that he stands upright and bellows, "Goddam God." The tactic is much more subtle — exerting on human beings a claim only God can utter; one that no earthly power may exact. It is a life and death command, seized on, expropriated by the state. God commands, "Thou shalt not kill" — but the state commands, "Thou shalt kill." This seems, in any age, the clearest, most concrete form of the blasphemy John refers to.

"I saw another beast which came up out of the earth." The growth of the *imperium* is portrayed, the power now shows itself abroad; irresistible, omnicompetent, omnipotent, omnivorous, omnipresent. "It had two horns like a lamb's but spoke like a dragon." (Rev. 13:11) It has the characteristics of both the first and second beast, patched together.

The offspring of the dragon and the beast wields authority granted by the beast. A kind of unholy spirit, he proceeds from the Dragon, who rose from chaos, from the sea. He proceeds also from the son figure, who comes fully accoutered, accompanied by a panoply of institutions, from the earth. This unholy one acts in the name of a dark "other," the unholy spirit of the beast. Its destiny is to be a stalking shadow, a mouthpiece, to electrify the public, to inject the bestial spirit, to amplify his master, a sort of infernal press agent.

"He made the earth and its inhabitants worship the beast." (Rev. 13:12) A kind of anti-scriptural statement. Jesus says of the Holy Spirit: "He will teach you all truth." (Jn. 13) Here, another sort of spirit teaches all falsity, all deceit, all propaganda; his task is simple; a political one, the "puffing" of the beast, the enslavement and blinding of citizens. "He led them to worship the beast whose mortal wound had been healed — and worked great miracles, making fire come down from heaven." Jesus had often spoken of the false miracles of the anti-Christ — the false prophet. By the miracles it is allowed to perform, it deludes. As the Holy Spirit teaches truth, this one teaches lies, unreality. "And finally it made them erect an image in honor of the beast that had been wounded by the sword and yet lived." This anti-Spirit always serves another, points to another. It does not erect a statue or image of itself; it refers its glory and worth back to the beast: a subaltern, an impeccable civil servant.

A great truth is inverted in the service of untruth. The Christian tradition has no images of the Holy Spirit. The Spirit points to another. He leads us to the truth of the Son and the Father. Here, in a kind of horrid parody, the people erect an image, not of the anti-spirit, but of the anti-son — the anti-Christ. Moreover, this image is wired — a kind of ventriloquist. "It was allowed to give breath to the image to be put to death." (Rev. 13:15) The image speaks back to the people, exactly what they want to hear. It has no proper ego, no proper existence; but it is extremely sensitive to the public, their fear and despair and ambition. It is the perfect press secretary, speech writer, power broker, political mediator.

We are told that, in those times, one element of religion was magic, another was ventriloquism. The emperors built talking statues, who offered oracles on demand. One hears, too, an echo of an Old Testament miracle, "Fire came down ... to earth before men's eyes." (Rev. 13:13) Many elements of truth have been gathered, placed in the service of untruth.

Are there reverberations of our present plight? In periods of turmoil, magic and sorcery, numerology, astrology, ventriloquism, all become ingredients in a brew of pseudo-religion. People are uneasy with traditional religion; it seems to have lost its savor, its symbols break up. And especially, when people are invaded by a kind of machine mentality, magic becomes crucial. They want results. The machine promises its own kind of magic — quick returns, cheap grace, instant miracles. People long to have life set in order; and quickly. Why not? The gods are machines like everything else. The Romans carried the machine-god ideal to its cynical last stage; public dramas often ended with a god settings things right; *"deus ex machina,"* literally, a god from the machine. Someone backstage worked the winch; down would come the divine one on wires, things would shortly be righted. Then the idol would be hoisted up again. It was a literal and crude version of popular religion. When things are messed up, God must intervene, then disappear again into the empyrean. Things will be better!

The connection between the machine and the gods is a very ancient one. The game goes on today; a proliferation of magic, people looking to the stars, even to the devil — by the millions, we are assured; employees and generals and researchers, turning to the gods of war.

The times make all this almost inevitable. Traditional religions are sunk; only here and there, small communities retain, survive, hidden, dislocated, obscured by official religion. Such communities are quite rare; as rare, indeed, as they were in the first centuries.

Then, too, political life is in chaos. Impossible to make sense of the senseless chatter, the trivialities, the downright lies. And the economic squeeze is on. Everything breaks up: marriages, friendships, the delicate balance between yin and yang, the world without and the world of spirit. People lose confidence in the simple power of good work, of being able to "make a difference." That plaint, which was once connected with physical disability, or with age, is now common to all — to the young, students, workers, young parents. They feel helpless, abused, worked over, expendable, trapped. It is rarer each day to meet with a young person who feels the world goes right for him or her, that he or she is making a contribution, doing good work.

Magic is the way out — when the way in, the simple equation between good means and worthy end, between good work and spiritual satisfaction, has broken down.

In contrast to this subtle and vicious interplay of frustration and magic, a kind of boxed-in, directionless pressure, one thinks of "mystery"; an ancient reality in every religious tradition.

We use the word rather loosely, of an experience that lies outside our understanding. But the Bible grants it a precise meaning. Paul calls Christ, "*the* mystery." Divine and human, He sums up all reality; the reality of God and human life — the known and accessible — and at the same time the unknown, and unreachable. In Him we have both distance and access to the Father, distance and access to human life.

How does Christ's activity differ from magic? Are the words, relics, bread and wine, the water in Baptism, the oil in the sacrament of the sick something more than manipulated symbols? Is it possible to use these things other than magically? Or is the expectation merely that one will perform this or that act, and obtain some immediate infallible, visible benefit?

In magical activity, a power is invoked, drawn to the human scene unfailingly, in consequence of certain formulas. Say these words, do this; relief will be offered. One can, beyond doubt, with the mediation of this or that object, word, gain access to power. The ouija board will speak to me. The stars will answer. With numerology I can unlock the future. But in such cases, what happens to the "believer"?

Here we touch on the basic difference between magic and worship. Magic allows one to remain totally unchanged, even while the god is put to service. The genie appears, is put in harness, enters my employ, as the Romans dramatized. But he leaves the human scene untouched, unchanged — unless we grant, in some cases, worsened. The transaction demands no change of heart. One can be as cruel, selfish, lustful, thoughtless after the magical activity as before. (Interestingly, the Bible seldom uses the word magic — it prefers to call such activity idolatry. Implying that the magical practitioner is in bondage to false gods, in fact is anti-religious.)

"Mysterious" activity could be understood in many ways: prayer (in the Christian tradition), sacraments, communion. Such acts are in principle worlds apart from magic. For mystery presupposes a willingness to undergo change, conversion, rebirth, death itself. One submits to the mystery, rather than manipulates it. (This is a classical view of things, a kind of ideal. One could hardly claim that Christians invariably act this way. We are as infected with magic, magical hope, magical religion as anybody — but, the supposition in scripture and the tradition is other.) Those who turn toward the true God are required to turn away from ego, from sin, from the encased selfishness in which they habitually walk. If we celebrate communion together, if we are baptized into a community, we submit to rebirth, declare our willingness to suffer, to work for justice, to include the neighbor in our conscientious regard for the world — to get reborn finally. Only at this point do we win access to the Divine.

We win it only because He graciously grants it. This is another difference between the two realities. In magic, the initiative is human — I undertake this work and carry it through, and the god submits, gives in. In mystery, God takes the initiative. The first invitation, the first summons, is on His part; the human action, rightly understood, can only be a response to Him.

In the Beast image, the concentration is totally upon magical activity. The beasts stalk at large because we want them around — they are our medicine, our idols. Thus the beasts enlist people into idolatry, into magical activity, to the degradation of mystery.

The passage is also a stern unmasking of the "freedom" the world hopes for and the beast promises. Every promise leads in the same direction: stupefied minds, crowds that are absolutely ruthless, in bondage to the beasts; "the whole world followed after." The promise of freedom that underlies magical practice, turns out to be a bait in a trap. The trap closes, the people are enslaved. The bestial magic was desperately enticing; people sought freedom from the complications of this world, from its iron claims. But they only succeeded in enslaving themselves more deeply.

Translated today, we see more magic, not less; the folly that declares, with bigger and better technology we can rid ourselves of the ills of technology. In place of beasts, we concoct and worship bigger beasts. We bring home the technology perfected in Vietnam. Now anti-personnel weaponry is put to personal and social use (a close translation of this chapter). The itch is in the air; the way out of the impasse of violent technology is more technology, which, perhaps, somehow, against all logic, against all sanity, will turn us peaceful.

Perhaps having murdered so many, we can now exorcize the beast, using the same machine, bloodstained as they are (the same minds and hands, bloodstained as they are) on behalf of human need. But can machines save or help, once they have been put exclusively to uses to death? Can minds be healed, polluted with violence, possessed by the quackery of technique? Will not something entirely unexpected occur — our delusions get us stuck in the gears and guts of two beasts instead of one?

The effect of idolatry on the community is, of course, devastating. "The whole world went after the beast in wondering admiration." (Rev. 13:3) Awe, religious awe, fear, marveling. The impact is a hideous echo of the Psalms, the Prophets, Luke's Gospel, John's Gospel. Such an impact God had exerted; now the beast surpasses Him. "Men worshipped the dragon because he had conferred his authority upon the beast." (Rev. 13:4) The people shout and shout, like the demons who are their instructors: "Who is like the beast? Who can fight against it?" The answer is clearly implied: The beast is absolutely irresistible. Indeed, John does not balk at the bitter truth; he declares bluntly: "The beast was allowed to fight against God's people, and to defeat them...." (Rev. 13:7) Adore or die.

A worldwide movement thus grows around an idolatrous image. Signs and wonders, miracles, a stupendous following; things never promised to Christ Himself. No scripture ever bestowed on the messiah what the beast achieves so easily, irresistibly, with such aplomb.

Will there be universal adulation, acceptance, belief, at the appearance of the messiah? Judging by His treatment at our hands in the days of His flesh, the reception on the last day will follow an ominous pattern. In contrast, the promise of glory is made and fyulfilled abruptly at the appearance of the imperial state. A wondrous secular epiphany, a heyday of signs and wonders.

One thinks inevitably of events of our own lifetime: in Germany, America, South Africa, Russia, Cuba, China. At times, the state appears absolutely irresistible in the eyes of the masses, the intellectuals, the religious people. Such a fervor of enthusiasm builds up; only fools stand aside, and very few at that. Then they simply are made to disappear.

One is reminded of scenes in the Munich Stadium at the appearance of Hitler, or in Peking during the Cultural Revolution, or of the frenetic response to Castro by the crowds. Such occasions cut across all ideologies; they are also extremely dangerous, no matter from what source they arise. These pseudo-liturgies, frenzied, racist, sexist, fascist, orchestrated with deliberate care, quasi-religious even, manifest in every case, symptoms of mass seduction, loss of individual dignity, personality and conscience to "the leader."

It seems important to linger over the Beast texts; also, an enormous worldwide following is according — not to God — but to the state. We are clearly commanded to be suspicious of such events. The Bible indicates that when religion is invoked by the beast, jeopardy is doubled against the human spirit. One is consumed in a kind of religious fervor, at the behest of this or that authority or political slogan, catchword, ideology. And the object of all this is always the same: inevitably and simply, war. By way of contrast, the ground the Bible opens is quite modest, distrustful of the mass mind, of the sanctified leader, whom it calls, unequivocally (whether individual, symbol, source of authority and coercion), the Beast. Or in Bonhoeffer's words, "The leader who becomes the misleader."

The chapter proceeds; the third beast, the Unholy Spirit — works great miracles, makes fire come down, "...deludes the inhabitants of the earth, made them erect an image in honor of the beast that had been wounded." (Rev. 13:14-15) This Unholy Spirit breathes speech into the image of the beast, which is set up as the very type and ikon of creation. The beast can then ape God as judge, can concoct a kind of Final Day scene. All who refuse to worship him must appear in court. In a weird trial, conducted by a malevolent ventriloquist doll, this judge-image condemns the non-worshippers to death. We have a kind of parody of the 24th chapter of Matthew's Gospel, where Jesus describes in some detail the last judgment, and then sets up criteria for blessedness or damnation. Has one fed the poor, harbored the homeless, nursed the sick? But here we are offered a very different criterion for death and life. Do people worship the idol, are they fervent magic men? No mention is made of good works, no mention of compassion or response to human need; or indeed to their opposite.

> *It* [that is the image] *caused everyone, great and small, rich and poor, slave and free, to be branded with a mark on his right hand or forehead, and no one was allowed to buy or sell unless he bore this beast's mark, either name or number.* (Rev. 13:16-17)

Two sorts of punishment are inflicted by the Unholy Spirit, executed by the Unholy Son, on the refusers. The first is death, the second, economic sanctions. Those who resist simply disappear, in one way or the other. They die, or they are boycotted out of existence, out of citizenship. They may not function in the state. Their crime is essentially beyond pardon or remorse; they have refused to worship the state.

One thinks of the cost of political resistance across the world today. One or another example is pertinent but hardly exhaustive — one could speak of fifty countries where the consequences of political and religious resistance are torture, long prison sentences, economic sanctions, degradation, or death itself. In Russia, equivalent sentences of death are passed out against all dissidents but the very famous — sentences in slave camps and psychiatric wards. When the convicted finish one sentence, they receive another. Or they are sent to hospitals where psychiatrists experiment, inject, attempt to reduce the deviants to mere vegetables.

In another tactic, such people are reduced to the status of non-persons — as in the case of the poet Mandelstam. Human rights are wiped out, the convicted wander the country like ghosts, forbidden access to Moscow, without income, without jobs, citizenship papers. The punishment is a weird mingling of death and economic sanction.

It is undoubtedly too easy to declare that such crimes of the state are unknown in America. What the Russians dare against their own people, Americans brought down on Vietnamese — witness the tiger cages, the 150,000 political prisoners in South Vietnam at the end of the war. Because such atrocities are usually committed (on this scale) outside the US, Americans live be the delusion that official crimes are forbidden and abhorred by our authorities; they conclude that our political arrangements are quite humane.

In verse 16, John refers to a "stigma," a mark on the right hand or forehead. It means something like "grade-A meat." The state marks its victim-citizens, numbers and tags them. Soldiers wear dogtags. After the Attica uprising, bodies were rounded up, a tag was attached to their toes, they were shoved into drawers like dead beef.

When one is arrested and put in jail, he or she is also given a number. The offender, virtuous or not, is reduced to a thing, an object, a no one. One ceases to be of public interest — one is an item in a body count. This is a prime tactic of the state — to tag and number and stamp people.

The most important thing at a border crossing is not the traveler, but his or her "papers," which must be "in order." Most bureaucrats, as they mount the ladder, become shufflers of papers, instead of people-serving. In all such ways, human life is abstracted, filed, computerized, to the point where it becomes coercible, manageable.

It is difficult today, and rare, to imagine any important sector of our life unrelated to the state. Or to pursue an independent course in such a sector. Or, to serve this or that area of human need without recourse to the state. Where else indeed are poor people to gain medical aid, or decent housing, or education or transport, or a survival stipend? Can one enter a profession without state aid? How few are the areas of local or individual autonomy left to us.

The question even arises, can we be religious people, apart from the state? The question is not idly put. It arises because of the dependence of our religious institutions, our properties, schools and churches on the state. (In which institutions we presumably function as believing people.) The fact is, of course, that most such institutions exist free of tax burdens, because from the state's point of view, they are useful; they churn out good citizens. They also encourage a certain illusion of autonomy.

A French theologian, Jacques Ellul, asks us to look deeply into the creeping illness of omnistate activity:

> "To think of everything as political, to conceal everything by using this word, with intellectuals taking the cue from Plato and several others, to place everything in the hands of the state, to appeal to the state in all circumstances, to subordinate the problems of the individual to those of the group, to believe that political affairs are on everybody's level, and everybody is qualified to deal with them...." (*The Political Illusion*)

Presuming to "come of age" by technological wonder-working, we only succeed in prostrating ourselves before new gods. Not only does the state move to the center stage of life, we spontaneously and personally accept the situation. We believe that for the world to be in good order the state must have the final word, the life and death power, the peace or war power, the power to police, tax, act in secret, deceive, to exercize authority over us from birth to death. From the point at which a young child walks for the first time into a public school, he or she steps into a universe whose four walls are eloquent with certain suppositions about the future. The child does not enter a void at age five — he or she steps into the state. Teacher is paid by the state; the building is maintained by the state....

Finally, one enters a state university. There the dependence is more evident than ever, with some eighty per cent of the ticket paid by public funds. We may consider that faculties and students are in a rather more sophisticated, human situation than the poorhouse wards in Victorian England, where brutes in gray aprons spooned out skinny soup once a day. When one of the beneficiaries, an infamous ingrate named Oliver Twist, asked for more, all hell broke loose. The method is much more civilized now. But who isn't lining up for soup?

Invisible writing, footnotes on our conscience. If one is seeking a benefit, one had show capacity for gratitude. If one is offered a ticket to the middle class, quasi-free, or at reduced rate, how can he complain about paying taxes? Or about drafted in the next war?

It becomes more and more difficult to imagine alternatives to such a system, since the system is so all-encompassing, all but spiritualized, immobilizing to the imagination. Economically speaking, statism often takes the form of preempting one's future. The majority of college students owe money to the state for their education. The majority of home "owners" are in debt to the banks. Such indebtedness sets one's future along a strict line: the future of individuals, of families, of politicians, into a certain line of conduct. Dissent becomes less and less likely; mouths and minds close like bank vaults — or like tombs.

Is it true that state worship is no longer demanded of us? People are enraged when one draws analogies, which, to John, seemed terrifyingly apt and natural. We are heirs of a longer political history, we are children of the separation of throne and altar. Or so it is said. But in the baleful light of modern war, subversion of human rights, torture, prison without trial — and over and above all that, the subversion or silencing of the churches, the question indeed lingers in the air: Has not Rome's idolatrous invasion of the sanctuary occurred again? Is there a notable difference, after all, between offering a pinch of incense to the emperor's image, and marching off to his wars? One might justly say that Caesar has merely secularized his control; his statue is not in the churches, one is free to worship true God. This, however, is not the question before us, which cuts deeper. The question is the claim over life and death, uttered by the Beast; a claim of domination which simply runs counter to the existence of God.

The biblical tradition urges us to shrink our fealty to the vanishing point. Jesus says coolly, "render to Caesar, render to God." He leaves the matter abruptly to us. But what did He render in both cases? Very little in one; everything, including His life, in the other. He by no means recommends a 50/50 proposition — give Caesar and God equal parts of fealty. He says, in effect, "Give Caesar next to nothing." Fling him a coin now and again, if you can do even that in good conscience. And then render to God what is His due — which is to say, your life, being, heart's devotion.

Where are our hearts today? What do we "follow after"? The gods of modern life are indeed a weird mix of artifacts, attitudes, visions, ambitions, weapons, the bloodline, the nation, the church, money, ego, sexual muscle, pride of place, security, violence; all tributes to the ultimate power of death. Such atrocious power this demonic reality is granted — granted, when all is said, by us! Power embodied in machines of war, preparation of war, the stockpiling of nuclear weapons; more: in all images of violence and hatred; in the constant appeal to "national security," "defense"; in all inticements and divisions among people: competition, money, ego, self-aggrandizement. Contemporary life creates a veritable pantheon of idols, an iconography before which men and women willingly, fervently, despairingly bend the knee.

The idols decree that the worshipper himself must die. This is implicit. The overt message is: "All who would not worship the image are to be put to death." Worship or die. But also, worship *and* die. On the one hand, everyone outside the circle of worship is to be put to death. But the passage raises the question: What happens to those within the circle? The implication is that they have already embraced death. They have taken the idol into their arms; it has suffocated them.

And one must insist — this bestial worship is not pseudo-mystical or abstract. It is a practical matter of human values, of where the money goes, where it comes from. A matter also of attitudes toward the church and state. Most people attend "the church of their choice" just as they vote for "the candidate of their choice." They enter a quasi-religious, quasi-political fog, to freshen up illusions, to be reminded, nudged, nurtured by the "idols of their choice." Indeed only rarely do religious people raise such questions as where our hearts are, where our idols are, what we are truly worshipping.

The triumph of the technological super state is thus to make of religion another gear, a lubricant in its machinery. In fact, most people look to religion merely to reinforce the values of the culture. That is to say, to dust off on Sunday or Sabbath the idols they live by during the secular, money-chasing, morally dubious week.

Idols: money, success, violence, racism, sexism, years of silence during the Vietnam War, Southern churches across half the United States choosing and rejecting worshippers on Sunday like a vile flea market, the hour in church being the most segregated hour of the week. No gospel breakthrough. In sermons, personal salvation exalted, a cozy domestic ethic of home and hearth and the bloodline — another idol; the denial of the social nature of salvation as taught by the Bible.

In vivid, even bloody contrast, Revelation opens up a deeper level of experience. It suggests that events, good and bad, horrors, political systems must be taken into account, must be taken seriously. More, Revelation implies a truth the world can never accede to; something other than its own process is taking place. A spiritual judgment rests on the crimes of policy: military, economic, diplomatic.

The beast does not have the last word. Nor do his idolaters, the deluded technological idol-makers and adorers, the harassed, eternally and childishly hopeful keepers of the political and military shrines.

Yet this "view from above," if you will, is not merely a word of judgment. It is also a word of reassurance and love. Chapter 14 of Revelation might be called the Taming of the Beast; it puts him in a cage, a larger reality. The celestial scene suggests that death is not the final fact of life; nor do the lords of death have the final word; the death dealers, the war makers, the misogynists, the racists. A reality, deeper, more lasting, joyful, persistent, surges up — "the Lamb and the faithful."

Death is not the final word; Love is. Or fidelity. Or the peaceable kingdom. The community in its dreadful last-ditch combat needs this assurance. The Beast episode may, in other words, offer a startling, piercingly exact vision of the course of the world; but it offers very little relief. Are we stuck fast in evil? Or is there something else? The book says there is. It constantly relieves the horrifying truth of history with a deeper, more hopeful truth of history. Which is to say, God is still God. And death, to which the idolaters pay a tribute of victims, is not the final word. His bloody hand is stayed.

Revelation is thus more than a particular intuitive view of human events. It offers not just an accurate, devastating image of history, a conclusion we might reach, if we read and marveled at the Beast image only. Certainly the episode offers a fascinating insight into the function and malfunction of power. But we are still justified in persisting; indeed we must persist in asking: What is the outcome? If it is true to God, as well as to human life, the book must offer two stages of understanding, not one. Truth of events, relief from events. Horror of the world, conscience in the world. And the two must not be radically divided. It is after all, in the world, in the welter of politics and history, the tangled crimes of our people and institutions, that we work out our salvation. It is also here that our salvation is granted (if indeed it is to be granted).

So the book rightly pays tribute to human responsibility; events really mean something. We cannot wash our hands, declare ourselves immaculate. We are stuck.

Then we are unstuck.

Much of what is called religion concentrates, today, on "God alone," a platonic view of the world. Invariably such a view is aligned with privilege, class, income. God must be served; implicit in the statement but never said, even in a whisper, is — God must serve us. And only a stutter away, we need never serve others.

Such religion grants no real solidity to human life and experience. It seeks what Bonhoeffer calls cheap salvation. If such a God exists, salvation is indeed cheap. If on the other hand, life is a constant bloody interaction between two realities — one rife with death, the other hardly born; if life is tragic, dramatic, a struggle whose outcome is yet in the breach — then salvation is costly indeed.

The relief offered in Chapter 14 seems at first glance esoteric, dull even. It is a scene of worship, a celestial liturgy. Here faith is vindicated — and martyrdom and tears. Faith is swallowed in victory. A majestic scene is enacted around the altar; elders, angels, the four beasts and the Lamb stand at center. And the great cry of "Holy, holy, holy," arises. And then silence in heaven for half an hour.

Song and silence, the opposite of the previous savage incantation ("Who is like the beast?"). The community speaks, even its silence speaks. (My word is myself; I speak it with a sense of responsibility. Its weight is burdensome. The word will return to haunt me, I am never done with its consequences.) And ultimately, when the gauntlet is laid down by the beast, the community stands firm. That is why in the Book of Revelation, the community is in perennial trouble. It has refused to incant the beast and thereby grant it an ever more inflated existence, the existence of Big Brother.

In modern life, by way of contrast, the word is commonly emptied of relationship, emptied of the substance of the speaker, emptied of life, emptied of deeds. We don't expect words to lead to deeds. Especially not in politics, advertising, economics. In contrast, John would recall us to the weight of the word, a word rendered weightless by political, indeed human, alienation.

The Beast episode is indeed a stark one; a bitter contrast to the prophetic community, standing by its word. The Beast speaks as he is given to speak; his master's puppet. Who then can hold him accountable for words which he never in fact spoke at all? He drew his personality, like a stream of darkness, from the job; he spoke words the crowds desired to hear, with all their intemperate hearts. Words were tossed out, alienating, duplicitous, hateful, blasphemous, contemptuous; and were lost in the air. They meant literally nothing; they were tokens of unreality. The people longed for a deity that would echo back their own emptiness, verify it, sanctify it even. So through their idol they were admitted to a secret; the essential emptiness of the word itself. They longed to be non-accountable; to be criminal without reprisal, to float in the moral void. And the Beast granted all this; he bestowed a seething, mindless, heartless character; freedom from the word as spiritual emanation, the word that bears one's pledge and vow into the world, the word that is ready even to be sealed in blood. But who wants speech to weigh so much? Intolerable!

The Gospel of John opens with a sublime clue to God's understanding of the Word: "In the beginning was the word." Then: "the word was made flesh." (Jn. 1:14) Jesus, the prophet, is the Word incarnate, the source of unity between word and substance, between word and martyrdom. So He will ultimately destroy the blathering beast. The word is creative, rather than empty or meaningless. One reflects on the degradation of the word in practically every phase of life today; then, on our responsibility to restore the word. By silence before speech, by forbearance, by honesty and courage and a sense that God's judgment weighs upon every word uttered by the living. (Matthew 12:36)

Seven Bowls of Wrath: Come Let Us Eat and Drink, for Tomorrow We Die

> *After this, as I looked, the sanctuary of the heavenly Tent of Testimony was thrown open, and out of it came the seven angels with the seven plagues. They were robed in fine linen, clean and shining, and had golden girdles around their breasts. Then one of the four living creatures gave the seven angels seven golden bowls full of the wrath of God who lives for ever and ever; and the sanctuary was filled with smoke from the glory of God and his power, so that no one could endure it until the seven plagues of the seven angels were completed.* (Rev. 15:5 ff.)

After the seven seals (the revealing of the true forces moving history), the seven plagues (the unmasking of disguises), now come the seven bowls.

We are not told what the bowls contained, the ingredients which loosed such catastrophe.... A general formula is offered, a recipe for all seven; "filled with the wrath of God...." His anger sets the world aflame.

The image corresponds vividly to our bad will; our placing the burden of adversity, disasters, on God. When things go well, we congratulate ourselves; when they go ill, we have a scapegoat — a divine one. This is commonly known as the yin and yang of civil religion. Anything less civilized, less religious, could hardly be imagined.

The wrath of God is in fact the lees of our crime. His wrath is the wine of these bowls — sour and potent. It pours out on the earth, the moral equivalent of our crimes, to wither, incinerate, set aflame, corrupt, toxify, induce drought and flood. The Bible traces the entire path of crime, from its ricochet off human bone and flesh to its blind strike against the earth and its gentle order.

What sort of God, indeed, would be anything but wrathful at the crimes of the nations today? Let us not play fool. The bowls are brimming with the concentrated essence of human malice; neither sweet nor savory, the lees of life. And as the seals were broken and the trumpet was commanded to sound, so here, the bowls must be poured out. It is the summoning of those duplicitous ploys which would 1) commit crimes against the earth, its people, and God; and 2) mask the crime in high-sounding phrases, diplomatic politesse, abstract swabbing of the wounds of humanity. (I am reminded of a photo: The Secretary of State and the someone or other of Brazil are shaking hands over a new agreement, to share the spoils. The spoils are, or course, the tortured and exiled and imprisoned who resist the commissars. Thus another of those "hundred years of detente" which will rot apart in the next year or so.)

I like the act of obedience. The angel pours out the bowls, one after another, seven for seven. It is "calling the shots," an angelic office. Those hands must be of a singular purity and strength; the hands of ministers, of Christ, of God. The hands of truth, hands that serve the tongue that speaks the truth. The angel is Minister of the austere impalatable truth that "murder will out"; not blindly or automatically, but through those to whom murder is unacceptable. Murder will out in high places also; pretension must be brought low (where indeed it belongs), a kind of perfumed Mafia, an unaccountable credit card. The pretension must be brought low, an accounting. When the bowl is turned over on such mighty heads — what consternation, what flames bursting forth in the infernal precincts of the brain!

The golden bowls are also instruments of worship. They are borne out of the Tent of Testimony. In this tent Moses had access to God. Out of the Tent, out of God's mouth, issues the truth of life. That life is wrathful. Has He vomited into the bowls, is this the sour truth? "I will vomit you out of my mouth...." In any case, the fruit of worship is judgment, the truth aflame; ruin, chaos laid against the well-laid plans of the powerful. This is the way worship touches the world; to bring its values and pretensions down. A kind of anti-communion; not meant solely for the strengthening of the faithful, but a flame upon the earth — to hasten ruin, to go public, to assign guilt, to bring the millennial patience of God to term. To speed things up. In such a way, to declare an end also to those subterfuges which say: granted, we are doing a bad thing; still self-deceived and wishing to deceive others, we declare, we are not doing that thing at all, but something totally other. Which is to say, amid war and war preparation, we are acting beneficially, integrally, pro-humanly, ecologically, self-givingly, serviceably, etc., etc.

No, the bowl is poured out, the truth flares up; where smoke was, fire now is. I think of the angels as emanations of Jesus. His energies embodied, symbolized, at work in the world. Dignity, precision, truthfulness, clothed in gold and linen, resembling Him bent on His task, obedient and masterful at once; doing sevenfold what He does once and for all....

In somewhat this sense, He too is the "emanation," the son, perfect foil, voice, mind, truthsayer, witness, faithful one, image, ikon of the nameless invisible One who sits on the throne....

The procession moves out from the mysterious inner court, where no mortal is admitted. What transpires within is a pure work of truth and creation, at its fountainhead. The Son receives the word from the Father; indeed He is that word. The angels receive from the Son those bowls of concentrated anger (finally an essence of love outraged). Then at the doorway, the impalpable takes visible form, the celestial mystery meets the eye. Now it is clothed in metaphor, perceptible. It moves into the world. And the bowls are the precipitant of history. An inflammatory history smolders away while time lasts; justice is delayed, crime is scot free. But here, now, an end is reached. It flares out uncontrollably, the bowls are emptied.

And suddenly, all nature turns against those who have violated nature. Those who wore the mark of the Beast now carry that mark as a sore, a lesion, a disease.(Rev. 16:2) Those who poured out the blood of martyrs see the waters of the earth turn to blood. Living things die; presumably men and women die too. (Rev. 16:3) (They always die; that is a commonplace of history; what is new and strange is that now the sentence is turned against the killers.)

The angels of earth raise their voices in praise of the actions. So do the dead, those who earlier complained about the delay of justice against those who destroyed them. (Rev. 6:9, 8:3-4) Deep waters here! One thinks of the common agreement in the church and elsewhere, that no one dare voice approval of divine vengeance. Even where the wrath of God might be discerned (something rare indeed) His justice is strictly a forbidden topic. There is no judgment on His judgment.

Indeed, the exact opposite occur when things go badly. God is "blamed" for our misfortune; the bowls of creation ought really to be filled with blessings for such a blessed people!

Yet here something else occurs; a majestic judgment puts to flight such childish fretfulness. The four living creatures hand the bowls over; they are the spirits of nature. (A kind of animism, natural forces charged with spiritual meaning.) Indeed these "living creatures" are lent the dignity of the evangelists themselves, announcing the good news not only about humans, but from within all creation, imminent to the world. We must bear with that troubling vision. According to Revelation it is the whole cosmos, the living, the lowly, even the dead, who will judge us.

The bowls are given to the angels. These are also seen as guardian spirits; a delightful tradition tells how they intercede, listen, are patient before the querulous, complaining, cursing humans; how they intercede between us and the divine. Here, however, they have a different, more disturbing function; they hand us over to justice. They are unmasking servants, actors, miming our fate, dramatizing events; forces of goodness, pressing hard against a wall of evil. The unveiling of crime and punishment becomes a liturgical ceremony. Acting out the misuse of the earth brings the crime under divine scrutiny. The crime is interrupted, even in full progress; the criminals are brought to the bar. The crime will not go on forever, unavenged, before an indifferent God.

Does He see? Does He hear? Is He indifferent? Are we in the power of a celestial amputee, a ghost rider? The procession puts it all together. Here come His servants, the angels, in judgment. They are bent on destruction — and eventual restoration. All at once, the seven eons of human existence, inhabitation — misuse, ripoff, pretended mastery, pretentious stewardship, real destruction, the incursions of technology, the hatred of life that hid behind a facade of justice and right order and "human development" — these are ended. The angels are testing the earth. They are by no means offering an apology for God; if indeed God exists, we feel, He ought to be above all that. No, they are His ministers, not ours. It is our existence, our conduct, that are placed abruptly in question.

Could the ironic gift-bearing procession of the angels bear comparison with nonviolent symbolic activity today? I think of the series of draft file burnings that marked the Vietnam War years. At Catonsville, in New York, in Michigan, California, Chicago, Evanston, Hawaii, Rochester, Buffalo, in many other places, procession formed, a liturgy was enacted — to show that these papers were, in fact, inflammatory, obscene. A kind of anti-book burning took place, a burning away of ignorance, a purifying of hatred. A balancing of books.

In a liturgy, someone stands to the side to explain things, to engender understanding. Worship can never exist in esoteric isolation; it is for the people, as the Greeks understood. Thus, in the course of the pouring, an angel speaks; so, mysteriously, does an "altar."

> *I heard an angel of the waters say: just art thou in these judgments, holy one who are and has always been; for they shed the blood of your people and prophets, and you have given them blood to drink. They have their desserts. And I heard the altar cry: Yes, Lord God, sovereign over all, true and just are your judgments.* (Rev. 16:5-7)

A bitter comment indeed.

We are shaken in our false image of angels, formed by childish art. This one is no sexless patsy, afloat uneasily at the edge of creation, hovering between flesh and spirit. This is a majestic advocate of God, an advocate of outraged nature, the voice of creation, the prosecutor, the destroyer; "It was just; they are given blood to drink, for they poured out the blood of the innocent." (Rev. 16:5-6)

The fountainheads, the springs of the earth, have turned to blood.

A monstrous abundance of blood courses over the earth, the rivers and streams are like opened arteries. Now there is no water, only blood, apt image of the death of "all the just, from the blood of the just Abel, the blood of the prophets...." (Lk. 11:51; Rev. 18:24) The death of the innocent has become a literal carnage, it is enacted with wholesale savagery. Surely such horror makes the cry of the angels the only response befitting an outraged God, a violated universe. Thus the angelic cry, one of fierce anger, a just wrath; he rages, and not only on his own behalf; he is the reflection of that Other, the holy Conscience of the universe.

Then something equally dramatic. The stones of the altar ("living stones") are wrung; the blood of the martyrs has anointed them, the voices of the just ("How long, sovereign Lord, holy and true, must it be before thou wilt vindicate us and avenge our blood on the inhabitants of the earth?" Rev. 6:10) A cry arises from them, for vindication. Now the time of "patience" is over. The dead seal the verdict, judgment, with their living approval. It is a long sigh of "thank you" to One who would not leave them forever outcast, judged and condemned by Babylon.

When His passion neared, Jesus said to those who objected to the truth: "If these [my disciples] are silent, the stones will shout aloud." (Lk. 19:40) Can we not believe it? Today, the very stones shout out; the stones of prisons, of back alleys where the poor languish, the stones that are flung by the despairing.... What stones of the earth are not anointed with the tears and blood of victims? What stone is not an altar stone, a living stone? The mute are silent, the deaf unhearing; but creation tells the truth — our crimes are written on stone tablets.

Groups of Christians have held vigils at the Pentagon; at times, human blood, our blood, has been poured over its pillars. The stones retain the truth; after the most assiduous scrubbing, the shadow of blood remains. Thus for the first time, that monstrous temple appears as it is in truth, before the world, before the God of history, a place where crimes against humanity are planned and implemented, a temple whose very stones ooze with the sweat and blood of victims. Is it to be thought strange that this text, the stones that shout the truth, comes to mind, as we too strive in whatever clumsy way, to dramatize the truth about nuclear war, so well hidden? As we summon the ghosts locked in closets and planning rooms, silenced by a diabolical Pentagon liturgy, fed their bowls of blood like the idols of Baal, in the unspeakable Meditation Room of the Pentagon?

Truly we stand before a temple of Babylon.

Babylon will appear later as mercantile queen, port of the seven seas and their ships, teeming market of every luxury under the sun, heaped to the brim with pride of life and love and civilized arts. She will be named summarily: the whore. Here is yet another glimpse of the dark pilings that uphold proud empire. The empire lives by the death of the righteous. They are unassimilable, they speak out, they reprove and denounce, they will not take the "second death" for their portion (translated as moral silence and worldly prosperity). They will not be silent before all crimes committed against others, the poor, the victims. Least of all can they be counted on to bear on their persons the mark of the beast. Therefore they die.

We would like to think that the empire is virtuous. Or that it can be; that it can be made so, converted so to speak by a large dose of civic virtue. This is the core of Niebuhrianism, or liberalism, the dream of lovers of civic religion. In such ways, both church and state teeter about, "explicating" the doctrine of the lesser evil; as though the Gospel ever commended the state to our serious attention, except as adversary; or as if the lesser evil were ever anything but evil.

Civil crimes, in this theory and practice, become mere peccadillos. The system is self-purging, an unpolluted spring turned to holy water by the divine favor. In the unlikely event that authority slips from its high place, now and then — the recovery is immediate, the secular covenant is not broken. Systemic crime? A fractured national consciousness cannot admit to it; yesterday's war, yesterday's lie, is today's cold omelet. The makeup artist restores the ravaged face of leadership; a steady eye, an unshaking hand, grasp the tiller of SS State; the ship is unsinkable, the prexy unflappable.

Crime in high places, crime as a matter of fact, calculated, weighed, approved, remains always (almost always) at a fairly tolerable level. The public pulse is taken by experts; they report it sluggish, inattentive, comatose; the mad surgeons may proceed to hack at the body, hardly alive in any case; the conscience registering only indifference, slackness.

What is this "tolerable level"? There is no prior tolerable level; no law governs it, determines its limits.

In regard to state violence, citizens are like holiday- goers at a country fair, watching an ascending balloon; the sky is the limit. High crime may go for broke. As audacity grows, so does the level of toleration.

The stages here are instructive. The people are first of all occupied (preoccupied) with violence; then literally possessed by it. Give them (us) enough of it, a surfeit of it, the capacity will grow, contain, absorb. Thus the imperial aim corresponds to the spiritual process; seizure of the earth, possession of the soul. The legions march finally, on ourselves. The wars come home.

Thus the theory of "benign empire" can hardly be called biblical. The empire (we have seen the insight before, John is continually hammering it home) subsists on death; death is its ordinary menu and method. World supremacy, control of markets, control of production, internal colonization, multinational ripoffs — finally and quintessentially, the mad race to arm the world; imperial supremacy is a demonic goal upborne, fed, inflated by "the blood of the just."

The word demonic is of the essence, in a biblical view. Forces beyond the human invade structures and render them subhuman. They declare war on life, while pretending to serve and enhance life. They increase the tempo of acceptable violence, seize upon the world and human consciousness, reverse the process of moral emancipation, enslave authority to money, lust, ego, death — all under a sweet cover of justifying lingo and logic. The multitudes hasten, the powerful beckon — to pay and exact tribute, to undertake and assent to destruction, to create and gaze on the artistic myths of national history, to concoct and gape at technological marvels of weaponry, to serve death, that is to say: acceptably presented, enhanced, glorified, melded with the national aspiration.

Consider by way of example the atmosphere of America in this decade. What indeed is the spiritual temper of our people today, the level of their hope, the range of their vision, the drift of their converse and silence, the subjects that occupy their minds, their religious longings? What energies can they draw on, beyond brute survival, when for some fifteen years they drank the blood of the common artery of humanity, their thirst fed by the fever of their own leaders? What is the moral consequence of a diet of blood, a bath of blood? The question seems to the fastidious, both horrid and intemperate; it is in fact a biblical question, it is raised here.

The answer is also implied here. Nausea, disgust, illness of spirit, lassitude, dim vision, an itch for further violence to justify violence already committed, complacence and silence about crime, a shrunken horizon of human possibility, crazy religion, lessened joy, lessened hope, less of everything beautiful and truthful issuing from the raped earth, the raped conscience — who has not lived in the plague, who has not been plague-stricken?

A bowl of blood is outpoured. It turns the springs of sentiment and love to very blood; blood shed like water, water turned to blood, blood drunk like water. This is the outer sign, the drama, the signal, the stirred waters of consciousness, the truth of hidden event. How else "catch the conscience of the king"?

Otherwise, the horror goes on forever; never challenged, never halted, never controlled. The wheel turns, we are chained there; the cruel and tormenting inversion of right order and process, it even takes on the guise of truth itself. The mad brain, the mad pentagon, the mad Blight House, they become our landmarks, they issue our scripture, they house our tradition, our gods, our prophets. Reality! They call themselves, American reality; and after that, Christian reality! Jewish reality!

To go mad becomes the first commandment of citizenship.

If fifty years (by conservative estimate) will be required to purify the waters and land of Southeast Asia from our plague of defoliants — how long before our own streams are purified, before blood will be requited, and the waters flow again? ... Waters of consciousness, waters of compassion, waters of rebirth? Meantime, a desert....

The last three plagues can only be called political ones; chaos, then collapse.

Then the fifth angel poured out his bowl on the throne of the beast. Darkness fell over the beast's kingdom, and men bit their tongues because of their pains; and they cursed the God of heaven for their pain and sores. But they did not turn from their evil ways. (Rev. 16:10-11)

What an aptly foul symbol for the divine contempt, rejection of the world-wielding claim of the bestial state! The throne was draped for great occasions, a sign of honor and captivation. The beast slumped there, comfortable in the cockpit of this world. He was in secure possession. But now, over the "seat of power," is dumped a bowl of incendiary filth. Once, this seat (now, Revelation says it is empty; has he already resigned and fled?) — it was incandescent; it was the anti-light of the world. That world drew its baleful light from the beast; he sat there, aping the God who sits righteously on His throne, in possession of the universe.

It is all over, curtains. The world is plunged in darkness.

The meaning of false light is real darkness. People had been led astray, first led and then misled. Now they are literally blind. No king (not even a beast for a king), no light of the (under) world. (Sol. 17:21) "Harder to bear than the darkness was the burden of men to themselves...." (Rev. 16: 10-11) It is a picture of the despair of hell itself, in this world, in time. The obliteration of false light has only served to worsen the human condition. A false light better than none? That hardly seems the message; rather now, in darkness, our true state is revealed; an irony dear to John's Gospel also. In any case, an apothegm; when the gods fail, God is in for it. The people blaspheme.

Is the Beast subtly content that, even in his absence, he lives on in his cursing disciples? Now that his throne is emptied, dishonored, he has by no means perished; he has found another way to survive, indeed, to multiply his presence. He literally "possesses" humankind. We will see him again.

In any case, John assures us that, contrary to the fantasies of popular religion, nothing has changed. This remains true though purportedly momentous political changes have occurred; ie. the empire has tottered, the throne is empty and fallen. But what does this add up to, in the eyes of God? Is He astounded, shaken? Does He "follow after"? — even in the sense that He would have us shaken by the evidence of bad news piled on worse?

The political turmoil and conflagration are nothing more than a heap of ash — the ashes of Babylon, the ashes of the throne, put to the torch by an angel. The lights are out, they cannot be rekindled. All the hustle and fury of civilization moils about in the darkness, feeding on itself. What it was, it remains: an anthill of the self-condemned. Moral change? Not a feather weight is added, not an iota subtracted. People are what they were, their light was moral darkness; their darkness is — themselves.

In the arsenal of divine truth, there is no more blasting, devastating bolt loosed on the mind than this cool statement, twice repeated here, many times elsewhere. After Hiroshima and Nagasaki, after My Lai, after Chile and the Philippines and Korea, after some are incinerated and others experimented on, after the burning and flaying and bombing; "They [that is, we] only cursed the name of God who had the power to inflict such plagues, and they refused to repent or do Him homage." (Rev. 16:11)

Darkness. In John's Gospel, as the hour of death nears, Jesus draws His disciples together for a final *agape*, a meal of love and farewell. He indicates the presence of the betrayer, without betraying him to the others; a discreet gesture, a passing of food, a courtesy to Judas. Whereupon, we are told, Judas went out; to consummate his deal. And John adds, in a marvelous and laconic understatement, "It was night." (Jn. 13:30)

Thus here. The bowl of filth and fire is poured out over the throne of the beast, dishonoring him, disenthroning him. And the throne itself, with its spurious splendor, is extinguished. The dark mine of hell is voided; has lost its core, its fuel. The kingdom is plunged in darkness. "Men gnawed their tongues in agony, but they only cursed the God of heaven for their pains and sores, and would not repent of what they had done."

We do well to tread softly, as we peddle theories and philosophies of human perfection, cultural optimism, platonic or Niebuhrian. It may be that we are tread-

The Nightmare of God

ing on the Bible. Like it or not (we dislike it intensely), one of the constant themes of Revelation is that of imperfectibility, corruption, rejection by God. Revelation is our psychohistory. There is that within us which, willingly and with undivided heart, embraces damnation — our portion, our self-inflicted judgment. With all our crooked hearts, we want the world and its forbidden fruits; we want it when the fruits are "sweet in the mouth and sour in the guts"; a diabolic scripture of our own and the demons' devising. We want the world to enjoy, the gods of this world to adore; in fair weather and foul, when they fail us and when they serve us assiduously; in health and in sickness, in degradation (inevitable) and in mastery (dubious).

Revelation pushes aside our vain hopes, brings us to the edge, invites us to look over, into the abyss. Imagine the misfortunes of Job befalling yourself; imagine the sweet cosmos turned to ash. Then, in this mirror of destruction, see your own image. Are you now a child of God, a creaturely chastened one? You are not; you are twice damned, self-damned.

Can we bear to look? We had sought comfort here; we were granted something better — the truth.

The Day the Empire Fell, and How, and Why

> *After this I saw another angel coming down from heaven; he came with great authority, and the earth was alight with his splendor. Then in a mighty voice, he proclaimed: Fallen, fallen is Babylon the great! She has become a dwelling for demons, a haunt for every unclean spirit, for every foul and loathsome bird. For all nations have drunk deep of the wine of her fornication; the kings of the earth have committed fornication with her, and merchants the world over have grown rich on her bloated wealth.* (Rev. 18: 1-3)

What does it mean to dwell in Babylon?

The first fact about such a predicament is a simple one: Most people do not know they are there. The truth is hidden from them; they think they dwell in New York or Paris or Rio or Johannesburg; they know only cultural or national points of geography. A false sense of themselves keeps the truth at a distance.

A second fact follows. One does not know where he or she is; one probably does not know who he or she is. One is lost in what John calls the "second death."

Then as the city comes down, as the ruin looms (not usually on the moment, but more slowly — not as Hiroshima went, but as New York goes), one winks and blinks along with it all. Those who are ruined are the "good citizens" of normal times. Their special interests have both created and sustained the empire. Now in the moment (or the century) of ruin, not knowing who they are, knowing little of the judgment of God, against all odds, against the tide of history, against God himself, they continue to "believe in America" (or some other imperial entity); they shore up the fading mirage, at all costs, by every means.

Those who dwell in Babylon do not know they are there. Every age, every empire shares in this blindness. The citizens invariably regard themselves as different, unique, beyond social criticism. Such are the themes of propaganda, myth, even religious teaching: "Our people are a special case, our motivation is beyond question, we deserve the best of this world, our enemies stand self-condemned." The sustaining of such nonsense, its care and nurture, is of course no easy or simple matter. National myths have to circulate in a thousand ways, get heard, talked about, blessed; then they are passed on to children, touched up to a heroic degree, given finally the stature and form of dogma.

An example of such a myth is that of a "national covenant." For two centuries of American life, the covenant has assured Americans of a protected, quasi-permanent status in the world; it has made of us "His People." In seizing the land, in affluence unbounded, in quest and conquest, in shady means and ends, the myth has made us, sustained us, mystified us, put us, as they say, on top. Most important, the covenant is sealed with the Almighty himself; could there be a more prestigious and beneficent co-signer? O happy people! Now we may stand outside history (as well as direct it from within); we are literally Olympians, beyond criticism. And to us, the people of the covenant, other arrangements, other myths, appear in their true light — a lesser light, to be sure, the fate of lesser peoples.

Most Americans cannot imagine another way of understanding the national future and patrimony. Not to be first, on the roll call of weaponry, economic clout, gross national product, etc, etc? Quite literally, either we are first — or we are nothing; unimaginable to ourselves, incomprehensible, to friend and foe.

Any other status, a more modest place in the universe, is beyond imagining. The situation is, of course, two-edged. What we cannot imagine, we can scarcely bring to pass. Even if we wanted another way, even if the constant pollution of political (and religious) language were not drumming the theme at us: arrival, perfection, biggest and best, His people.

For those who have arrived, there is, of course, nowhere to go. Hence our sclerosis, impoverished imagination, strangulated energies and half-hearted talk. People carry the look of "those who are without hope." The covenant may be breaking up, it may simply be canceled; or, on the other hand, it may be hardening its terms, calling in its debts, literally condemning us to death, a mailed fist on our shoulder. No one seems to know which of these is happening, or even to care. Either outcome, interpretation, image, seems equally bearable, or equally unbearable. All is the same. The people have arrived, there is nowhere to go. There are no political alternatives, no new faces, no new words to tell of our predicament. Hopelessness, weary endurance, spoiled hopes, this is the look of our decade, of our people — most strikingly of all, the look of the young, who were inducted at birth into the covenant, and spent their early years being socialized into its mysteries. Today, they bear the stigma of our common dying — before they have fairly begun to live.

Are we fulfilling the old biblical image of Empire? According to the Bible, the history of empires is a network, vast, dreary, chiastic, of moral cliches. Empires are like aging spiders, limping on, weaving the same old ragged webs. They know only one thing to do, they secrete one pattern in their guts.

They act not so much out of enterprise (even killing enterprise) as out of dying instinct. Killers, even in their last days; what else is there to do?

To its builders, maintenance men, sycophants, rulers, torturers, slave-holders, Babylon is the bustling, hustling Empire in action; how to exploit, slay, aggran-

The Nightmare of God

dize, enslave, inspire fear, make money, build, create and cater to appetite, seize on and consume the world. The blueprint, hauled out and dusted off, is that of Egypt, Tyre, Sodom, Rome.

But the prophet knows something else. Judgment, clear lines of drawn, landmarks in time, non-assimilation of conscience. A warning is issued, a command to those citizens who can read the signs, who worship another god than Empire, who would have no part in its crimes. Flee.

Still, the question haunts us. How are we to know we are living in the time the prophet describes? Is Babylon building up around us, enlisting us, counting on our love of law and order, counting us among the responsible tax-paying "good Germans"?

The question is wrongly put. It is not given to us to know in this way. (It is given to fundamentalists; but their point is not ours.) We are not dealing with calipers and test tubes, with surveys, but with analogies, clues, likenesses, a sixth sense of things drawn from common understanding, tradition, accepted symbols. With what have been called, with some reason, "matters of faith."

Our instincts in such matters are worth trusting. We ponder the Bible, we look around us. A sense, an atmosphere makes itself felt. We sense that all sorts of people are undergoing a mysterious, creeping malaise. Perhaps it is just that common, hardly bearable, wasting illness that we should start from.

When people unload their burden, when they trust someone enough to speak up, it all comes out; one and the same look in their eyes, one feeling at the pit of their gut; free-floating, undiagnosed, hard to pin down. Something wrong, awry, the world off kilter. Something desperately wrong, at the heart of things; a sense that life is failing them, though it is not their fault, they have tried their best. A sense even, though everyone tries, though people are basically decent and peaceable — that nothing works really, for anyone. Thus the despair spreads; a social illness. Breakup; nothing holding, an ominous sense of remote tragedy nearing, impending a shadow over life, a bad dream at high noon.

These common soundings, this strange agreement on bad news, is by no means confined to the poor, to those at the bottom. Indeed it afflicts those who have least reason, were the world reasonable, to be touched by such a frost. I mean those who on any ledger can count on America working for them, making sense to them. They can touch their wallet, their bankbook, can travel, vacation, know leisure and its cultural uses, take stock of their securities; their family affection seems to be holding, their jobs pay off. On any scoreboard they would seem to be the winners.

It could even be said that the worst occurs to the fortunate; a cold sweat of anticipation. What then of the others, the majority? For them, life has stalled. Or it walks on, a nightmare, a horror. You see it in the dogged eyes of middle-aged professionals; long ago they lowered the bar on the high jump; now they tread gently and jump not at all. The big vaulting energies are in harness: to the job, to the mortgage, to the appetites and whims of children.

Surely it superfluous to flog a point which has become a needle, plunged in the brain. We live with it, we say — we mean to say — we are dying of it.

Greek tragedy offers a clue that seems to me valuable. In the drama of Oedipus, an unacknowledged crime has been committed, a plague lies on the city. There is only one way to be healed: The kind must come forward, confess and repair his sin. Only if he does this, can the city recover its health, and the people be spared.

In its treatment of the fall of Babylon, Revelation suggests a startlingly similar pattern. Babylon has overstepped itself. Its crime is beyond human measure, beyond tolerance of the organism. It is as though, morally speaking, one were to attempt to swallow a python whole, or to stop the tides of the sea in their tracks.

Eventually something explodes; a heart-stopping reversal in nature. The fabric of life rips apart, structures rot and fall, language floats free of reality, life makes less and less sense to those condemned to "live" it. A line has been stepped over, a taboo violated. The python swallows its captor, the tides drown the interloper.

This inhuman, superhuman (in effect, subhuman) measure of crime is a biblical expression for the common conduct of empire. The ascent to "number one" among the nations is a rake's progress. The crimes of those who seek power for themselves, for their institutions (for their church?), for their nation, grow progressively more grandiose, grotesque, indiscriminate. Crime drags along in the train of power like a squad of slaves captured on the road.

At some point, the slaves flex their muscles, and revolt. The high noon of the gods and of their sycophants is ironically plunged in twilight. The empire is no sooner secured, the borders pacified, the colonies subdued, then everything comes unstuck.

In accord with this sequence, the biblical sense of time is shockingly foreshortened. What matter a century or an hour, when the seeds of dissolution and violence are already sown? The proud creation of a thousand years is "judged in a single hour"... in that hour, all this wealth is laid waste."

The believers are given no choice; they are told simply "to flee." Another more detailed account of that flight, its disarray, urgency, poverty, is given us in Matthew's Gospel:

> "Then those who are in Judea must take to the hills. If one is on the roof, he must not come down to fetch his goods from the house; if in the field, he must not turn back for his coat. Alas for the women with child in those days, and for those with children at the breast! Pray that it may not be winter when you have to make your escape, or Sabbath. It will be a time of great distress, such as has never been seen from the beginning of the world until now, and will never be again. If that time of trouble were not cut short, no living thing could survive; but for the sake of God's chosen, it will be cut short." (Mt. 24:16-22)

Fleeing the doomed city, the burning catastrophe, is indeed a shattering image of a state of mind; alienation, self-distancing from crime and consequence. From crime, since one has determined not to live in complicity. From consequence, since one is mysteriously spared. Not spared in the crude sense that believers are exempted from the common destiny, however heroic they might be. But spared what John calls the "second death," whose atmosphere before the fact is despair, blindness, a shotgun at the shelter door; and after the fact, damnation.

Another clue to the time, the conduct required is to "be vigilant, keep watch." And again: "Read the signs of the times."

In Babylon, the signs are ignored, the people are morally comatose. They know events, they are not stupid, their leadership is skilled in the arts and dodges of survival, ploy, advantage. Leaders and citizens bathe in the light of imperial favor, they walk secure in the world.

Or so it seems. But the reality is something other. Suddenly (it is always sudden, this outcome) their lifeline is cut. No more plunder, profit, control. The covenant is revealed for what it was, from the beginning, a bargain struck, not with God but with the demons, the idols, with their own vainglorious lusts.

Their lament over the city is only the outraged, surprised cry of bad faith revealed. The covenant has broken apart. Now the lackey kings, the robber barons, the traitorous hucksters — they mourn neither the victims (whom they helped mightily to create) nor those who died in the downfall of the city (which they engineered). Not a tear, not a thought for the exploited and poor, whose flesh and blood they lived off.

First among the mourners: the political puppets, the colonels, the fascist underlings.

Such flourish today in the Third World, a noisome gang of slaves. They covet the junk rewards of the first and second worlds with all their craven hearts. Some of them, oil big-shots, call the plays — to a degree. As long as their enterprise and methods dovetail with those of their masters, they are allowed a certain leeway, whether in Israel, South Korea, the Philippines, Chile, Thailand. But let the climate change, the instructions from headquarters grow more explicit, the control more overt. In any case, their existence is provisional and edgy, governed by a very simple principle: They must be useful to the imperial powers. In a certain sense, they are, of course, indispensable. They give domestic legitimacy to a more subtle invasion — of markets, culture, social organization, the firm holding of military and ideological lines.

Their crime: betrayal of their own people.

Now they teeter on the edge of ruin. The ground under their feet is shaken — imperial ground, ceded by a duplicitous bargain. They "stand far off, in fear of [Babylon's] torment." (Rev. 18:10)

Well might they fear. In the smoking ruin of the empire, they read their own judgment, shortly to follow. Where can the sycophant go when Pharaoh is no more? He has no place to hide; his own people rise up in a fury; the mother country (more properly, biblically, brutally, "the whore") is out of business. So is he, and permanently.

Then there are the merchants, traffickers, bankers, wheelers and dealers. John gives a long enumeration of their wares, a helter-skelter mix of good, bad and indifferent; the deluxe, the necessary, the superfluous, a litany of human appetite, finickiness, frivolity and grandeur. His list of the goods and services of empire implies a kind of wonderment, even admiration, for such foibles. What a people — to want so much, to need so much, to consume so much! John is judging not only the masters of production, trade, merchandise, but the myriad appetites that handle, grab, bargain and pay up: the consuming public.

The city is the Great Consumer. It ends by being consumed.

Or could it be said, from another point of view, that it ended by consuming itself? Every good thing, every sign and evidence of civilization lay at its feet; it rode the saddle of the world, grabbed where it would, plundered, fed on the misery and death of others. And all the while it was putting the torch to itself.

Thus the irony that commands the threnody, its rhythm and tone; the double mind that knows and is ignorant, sees and is blind, both brings to pass and mourns the end of a cannibal era. The scene, scaled down to size, reminds one of a family of mourners, gathered around for the reading of a rich relative's will. Jealous of one another, murderously, politely competing, secretly hating the parent while he lived, concealing that hatred for cupidity's sake — now their lives are brought to a halt. The will is read; he has left them precisely nothing.

One can imagine the tone and atmosphere of such mourners in Babylon: bad faith, despair, sour-suppressed envy. "No one buys their cargo any more." (Rev. 18:11) Simple, final as that; the bottom has fallen out of the market; their tears fall like falling dollar signs.

The mourners, the deflated rich, keep a death watch for the imperial whore whose every whim had lined their pockets with gold.

We should not miss the tragic and special sense of the "goods and services" named here. The imperial merchants trade in literally everything. The market list goes imperceptibly from luxuries to food, to fauna — and then, to humans! "All kinds of costly wood, bronze, iron and marble, cinnamon, spice ... fine flour and wheat, cattle and sheep ... and slaves; that is human souls." (Rev. 18:13)

So inhuman a list of so-called human needs!

If consumerism is another name for the Great City, one cannot but add: what is finally consumed is — human beings.

We are told that Cyrus the Great devised a stunningly simple tactic to control dissent in his empire. The method was for domestic use only. Abroad, there were fire and sword for the rebellious. But at home, the King sedulously created a myth: largeness of mind, benignity, patient judgment of dissenters. The national climate was to be a delicate balance of public confidence and private terror.

So on given occasions, he held court, receiving the objectors, the injured, the dissenters. He heard them out, nodded sagely and sympathetically. Then, when the case was heard, the emperor would turn to the gigantic guards at his right hand and left, and speak a single thunderous sentence: "Eat him!" And in full court, the giants would set upon the victim, and eat him alive, conscientious flesh and all. No historian assures us that dissent flourished under this arrangement.

We have looked on the Great City as the Consumer, then as the Enslaver. She is also the Cannibal. Her list of goods and services, offered feverishly on the market, packaged, weighed, displayed, marked up, marked down, bejeweled, impoverished, for service, for pleasure, for hire, for sale — this list includes humans — it is consummated in the buying and selling of human lives. The victor demands the victim; the rich demand the poor; the system demands unemployment; the military sits hard on health, education and welfare; people make their living off people's dying; the weapons trade proliferates; we weave and encompass the earth with a lethal jacket of barbed wire.

Such a tangle of economic-political-military madness! We long to be done with it, we conceive in our minds another sort of empire — a virtuous one, in which a covenant was sworn in good faith, then kept unbroken. Alas, there is simply no evidence that such a dream is verified. The history of empires, according to the Bible, is a history of crime, duplicity, murder. The only breakthrough is offered by those who resist. Reform is a utopian dream; it only succeeds in making the empire more plausible, less overtly criminal, better adjusted to adjusted consciences.

No empire, warns Revelation, but makes of human lives its main provender, the coin of the realm.

But must this be, we ask? Can there be no virtuous empire? Cannot our own, the Great Society, change course, renounce its crimes, "learn its lesson," as the claim goes, after Vietnam?

The Bible offers only clues. And perhaps that terrible list of "goods and services," which ends by becoming a cannibal menu, offers such a clue.

Let the clue grow, until it becomes admissible evidence. Since Hiroshima, what flesh has been safe against the imperial cannibal? Since Korea, since Cambodia, Laos, Vietnam, El Salvador? We long to believe (and the longing is itself a measure of our cannibalization) that such crimes, excessive, repeated, constantly absorbed, explained away, justified, are no more than the "virtuous fault" of a virtuous people.

The karma of history — that daemon which waits, notes — is silent; according to Revelation, it takes the form of a patient, wise, implacable justice. All crimes are finally self-inflicted. There is no recovering from them, since in principle there is no repenting them. In this sense, the satraps and betrayers and murderers are correct, they read the times aright: "In one hour has judgment come ... has all this wealth been laid waste." (Rev. 18:17)

The countdown has begun. "A thousand years" may have been the boast of the empire; but "one hour" is the timing of God. That phrase "one hour," repeated three times by the bad-mouthing mourners, is their concession, deflation, surrender to judgment. In any case, not much time. (Not much time for believers, either.)

Twilight, a time of obscurity, a time when the most divergent readings are taken concerning the times, when clocks disagree and instruments go crazy. Let the money barons, the usurers, waste the final time as they will, scrambling to recoup their losses, mourning fruitlessly their spoiled game. But how are the noncitizens, the hardly-tolerated, the "off-scouring," as Paul calls us — how are we to live? What way, what instruction, what obedience, will be consistent with faith, evidence of hope, a sign and presence of love?

We have a day (or an hour) in which to "flee." The time is unimportant, except that it is short. It seizes on us abruptly, grants no place for backward looks, regrets, possessions.

This is the only instruction: "Come out of her, my people, lest you take part in her sin, lest you share in her plagues." (Rev. 18:4) An instruction worth dwelling on, at variance with prudence, forethought, common sense. Negative, the psycho experts would call it. Anti-cosmic, the Teilhardians would call it. Guilt-ridden, self-hating, the Essalin folk would call it. And so on, and so on. The word of God is fractious indeed, a source of cold comfort.

But it is quite possibly not the vocation of seers and divines to warm up that cold, to concoct a savory sauce for it, to render it palatable to human taste. Perhaps we are even meant to stay out in the cold, to put between the empire and ourselves whatever distance a single hour or a single day will allow.

In any case, though the command is not attractive, it is far from unexpected. We remember having heard it, or its like, before. It reminds us of the passage of Israel out of slavery through sea and desert; or it reminds us of baptism, ourselves drowned, resuscitated with the mouth-to-mouth aid of the Spirit. In any case, a stark primary symbol of death.

We cannot lightly say (though we long to say it): I shall remain in the empire, I shall be its child, its creature, its citizen. And I shall also be a Christian, in the midst of all. The statement implies that one has already shared the false consciousness of those who built the city up on the death, tears, slavery and extinction of others, all the while assuring themselves and the world (as they do today) that they bear no one ill will, that they are the most virtuous of peoples.

But what does it mean to "remain"; what does it mean to "flee"? There is some clue, I think, in the moral conduct and attitudes of some Christians during the Vietnam decade. They "fled," ethically speaking, even while, physically speaking, they remained. The uneasy balancing act, sustained only clumsily and partially, they called "resistance." They were haunted by the threat of God, His piercing sense of the crimes of the nation; "lest you take part in her sins; lest you share in her plagues."

Do those sins and plagues need enumerating?

The "goods and services" of the imperium are a vast catalogue of death-instruments. Compared to their variety, cost, ingenuity, the wealth of Tyre and Babylon is a nursery tale. To speak of weaponry alone, we devised for the world's delectation flotillas of arms that beggar the imagination: MARV's, MIRV's, MX missiles, Trident submarines, the neutron Bomb. Truly, the empire consumes people; the cannibal appetite grows by what it feeds on.

In face of all this, we are told, by the word of God, with utmost urgency, to "flee the plague."

When we refuse to pay taxes, to invest in our own and others' destruction, we are fleeing the plague.

When we stand outside consumer appetite and its junk culture, we are fleeing the plague.

When we tell the truth to our children and prepare them for the only adult world worth talking about, an adulthood of resistance against the warmaking state, we (and they) are fleeing the plague.

When we honor our professions by serving human needs instead of pandering to ego, folly, base rewards, we are fleeing the plague.

When we insist on hearing the truth in our churches, by speaking the truth there, challenging silence, inertia, worship as usual, we are fleeing the plague.

When we pierce the myths of the "virtuous empire" with the two-edged sword of God's word (ie. there is no virtuous empire), we are fleeing the plague....

The "shipmasters and seafaring men, sailors and traders" form another chorus of mourners. (Rev. 18:17) The fast buck, so to speak, has slowed; the winners are becoming losers, even in their own eyes. The umbilical that joined the whore to the colonies is severed "in an hour." "What city was like the great city?" They saw her from afar off; they saw many cities in their voyages; indeed, they laced together the cities of the world, erasing boundaries, ignoring distances, weaving the great myth more cunningly and tightly — "intercivilizing" the violent, satiating the covetous, renewing the jaded, puffing the myth that the earth, in service to human appetite, is literally boundless in its promise, and its delivery, of paradise.

And now, what their transfixed eyes behold is — hell. The city is burning.

A time of wreckage for those who wreck the earth.... (Rev. 11:18)

Then a mighty angel took up a stone like a great millstone and cast it into the sea, saying, So shall Babylon the great city be thrown down with violence.... (Rev. 18:21)

A gesture of immense power; the end of an era, a civilization. The great city falls by the weight of its accumulated crime. The waters of history close over, silence resumes; all sounds, human voices, music, the whir of machines, the night lights that signaled pleasure, celebration, the flourishing of arts ... all cease.

Thus a phase is passed; another judgment is rendered than that of the sycophants, time servers, investors and builders of the great empire. Heaven intervenes; the historic weight of sin, and the judgment of heaven, coincide. The city is down.

That stone cast by the angel into the sea; it lies there, gathering barnacles, heavy, inert, still precious, a relic, an artifact, not a mere rock out of nature. Another civilization will come upon it, dig it up, bring it to the surface, haul it to a new capital city, display it, wonder at it, reconstruct, speculate....

The response of heaven to the fall of Babylon is almost endearingly complex; it is also terrifying. The angelic finger wipes out, sets to rest, darkens, mutes, draws to a close, all evidence of human life and activity. The glory of the great city is quenched. Slowly, poetically, symbolically, the city turns to stone; the stone drops into the sea. The waters close over; it' is as though Babylon had never been. She is from henceforth no more than grist for the dustmill, a city under the sea, a lost Atlantis.

Then the angel commences a sublime dirge, drawn heavily from Jeremiah.

> *This is how the great city Babylon will be thrown down with violence, and will never be seen again. The music of harpists and musicians, of players of the flute and trumpet, will never be heard in you again. And the sound of the millstone will be heard no more. Never again will the light of a lamp be seen in you. No more will the voices of bride and groom be heard in you. Your business men were the most powerful in the world; with your false magic you deceived all the peoples of the world!* (Rev. 18:21-23)

It is a mournful chant of humanism violated, a chant with a sublime classic edge. A sense of fatalism; what must be, must be. A sense of sorrow for the ruin of a potentially sublime thing. How beautiful the city, its promise, the achievement of its arts and commerce! The angel is not part of the scene; he stands outside history. But he stands within, too; he is a mourner at the twilight of civilization.

Yet the element of anger, vindication, bloodshed is also present, and should be underscored if one is to share the piercing angelic sense of justice. A cosmic understanding; the scales of the universe, so long tipped in favor of imperial power, are about to be righted.

Two reasons are offered for the judgment passed against Babylon. (Rev. 18:23) The first is somewhat puzzling at first glance, the second is clear as a bloodstain. The light of the mind, the light of civilization, the light of public conscience; all go out — "because your merchants were the princes of the earth, and all nations were deceived by your sorcery." A combination of economic crime, and deception; the violence of property, the violence of diplomacy, the violence of war; a vicious triad that infected all peoples.

Sorcery, service of idols, magic, Satanism, slavery to the whore, adoration of money and imperial politics, secular religion, search for the civil savior — these are the themes of a judgment, under several images.

And the crimes cannot be contained; the violence spreads. The sorrowful truth is verified once more; the conduct of the great powers is immensely influential among other, lesser nations. The small nations want their share of the poisoned pie: international finance, colonization, prosperity, world markets. They bend ear to the susurrations in the corridors of power — the bargains struck, the deals made, the treaties of mutual aid or mutual hostility, the carving out of blocs and spheres of power. All this draws the nations in to the whirling mad dance. It all seems straightforward, civilly virtuous, a game for the civilized; it is in fact a "sorcery." Everyone wants possession of that magical bottle, the code that releases the beneficent genie.

The "uncommitted nations." The church as "uncommitted" to the great white lie; committed to Christ....

Because of the sorcery of power (the angel of judgment implies), even the most innocent, life-giving elements of the empire come down, are destroyed. (Instructive is the angelic grief, contrasted with the crocodile tears shed by the great ones over those vestiges of power going up in fire and smoke. Their tears are a pollution of lost gain; the angel mourns, with an ironic human sense, because even excellent things cannot survive the holocaust. There is a kind of surgical tenderness in the angel, in sharp contrast to the base grief of the covetous. They mourn because the goose has perished by fire; no more golden eggs.)

Then the heavenly scene opens; another contrast. The downfall of Babylon affects various witnesses — angelic, human — strictly according to what each saw there; filthy lucre, the mournful beauty of a lost cause.

The puppet kings saw their profitable vassalage ending, the merchants and hucksters saw the destruction of the great market — the banks, stocks, investments, real and unreal estate that supported the empire and created their enormous mercantile fortunes. It was left to the great angel, strangely enough, to sound a human note. Is this because humans are incapable of it, caught up as they are, in the shady business of empire?

In any case, a heavenly chorus, human, angelic, or both, sounds the most shocking note of all. A cry of triumph — "Alleluia." Bitter as gall, a cry of vengeance and vindication at once: "Salvation and glory and power belong to our God, for his judgments are true and just; he has judged the great harlot who corrupted earth with her fornication, he has avenged on her the blood of his servants. And once more they cried, 'Halleluia!' the smoke from her goes up forever and forever." (Rev. 19:3)

Who could wish to linger over this scene? It is too savage a clue to the heart of Christ. If even an angel mourns the fall of Babylon, how can eternity resound with exultation, a judgment on human glory?

The scene recalls us to the earlier one, the plaint of the martyrs, at justice delayed. (Rev. 6:9 ff) The cry of the just is for justice; the cry is noted by God, but the plaint is deflected. Justice, they are told in effect, is God's concern; but not within time. Indeed, even He cannot square the circle. There is no final court of justice in this world; there are only innumerable courts, of more or less injustice.

Set things right in a world whose main business is the multiplying of crime? Where is it to stop, cry the martyrs? When is payment to begin? When will our tears and blood be indicated?

Not yet. Not in time. Not until the end of things. Now, in the fate of Babylon, that former scene is less obscure. Crime is unmasked, cumulative. Judgment is announced. "The smoke from her goes up forever." Sodom and Gomorrah, Babylon, Rome — then, is the final kingdom of this world — ourselves? It is for us to judge; for us to know that in so judging (or in fearing to judge) we are also being judged.

In any case, the weight of crime is cumulative. Each successive empire seizes on the ancient crimes, dusts them off, justifies them anew, an eye to the main chance. Under this weight we lie prone, sunken to ground, our imaginations chilled with death, our "way of life" revealed for the way of death it is, our crimes turning us by day into zombies, by night into vessels churning with nightmare.

The National House is declared clean, swept and garnished; the stains of genocide are removed in a "war on dirt." Then seven demons enter and possess the house. And the last state of that nation is worse than the first, as the Lord has warned.

It is hard to remind ourselves of such realities. "On to the next horror," think the people, locked in the runaway vehicle. "On to the next military adventure," exult the generals, blind as bats, chattering like dolls with cassettes in their guts.

Babylon's moral life is not a passage from crime to repentance, but only from crime to crime. Ourselves? From no one do we hear, after Vietnam, "Remember, and repent." Only: "Forget, and forget." Thus, our history becomes a progressive breakaway from all restraint. The empire rides and flogs the four horses: death, plague, famine, war in her wake. And we call it civilization, sanity.

So far are we from a collective sense of guilt, responsibility, unrepaired crime. So far, on the other hand, from a sense of solidarity in goodness, virtue, love.

Christians have expressed this sense of delayed justice in the doctrine of the "general judgment"; the final righting of the profound and bloody rift in the universe, the primal "fault" that splits the world into camps, blocs, nations, races, religions, classes.

In Revelation, judgment comes down. Babylon sins, and sins again. Her existence became a classical "state of sin"; of repeated crimes against humanity. Then the *denouement*. Silence, passive acceptance, despair, the "no contest" declared by the guilty.

No sound from the city. Only a chorus is left to comment on the action; to mourn and exult. Earlier, the chorus spoke from a shadowy world, a kind of kennel beneath the altar. And God offered cold comfort; He counseled patience, a strange and bitter medicine, as we have seen. But now, all is changed. The "few," the bloodstained remnant of faithful ones, are caught up in a flaming vortex of justice, a chant of triumph. What a transformation! It is to the prelude to glory.

Once, they suffered utter defeat at the hands of the great; now, they are vindicated. Thus, the strange and savage cry: "Alleluia, the smoke of her goes up forever...."

No one on this earth dares raise such a cry. It belongs to another time, another world. On the tongues of mortals, within time, it would indeed sound bloodthirsty, vengeful. It can never be raised while time lasts, even by those who pass through this world without a blemish, witnesses to the truth.

Let them seek vindication. They must do so; it is a cry from the tortured body of Christ. Revelation gives not the slightest hint of reproof while the empire is still intact and justice so long delayed. But not delayed forever.

And meantime, they (which is to say, ourselves) hearken to a call; to endure, to stand firm.

The Feast of Carrion

> *I saw an angel standing in the sun, and he shouted aloud to all the birds that were flying overhead in the sky. "Come here. Gather together at the great feast that God is giving. There will be flesh of kings for you, and the flesh of great generals and heroes, the flesh of horses and their riders and of all kinds of men, citizens and slaves, small and great."*
> (19:17-18)

The passage is shocking in the extreme. It seems as though God has become a savage carnivore. We recall with a pang the gracious eucharist: "The one who eats my flesh and drinks my blood, has life eternal." (Jn. 6:54) But now, an antieucharist is announced. We recall also the lovely simile: "The kingdom of heaven may be compared to a king who has a feast for his son's wedding." (Mt. 22:2) A wedding feast is a foretaste of glory. But now it is the great ones of earth who make up the menu of a nightmarish orgy. What can this mean?

A cosmic principle is at work here. The karma of the universe demands some final righting of wrongs. This is the law of the ecological web, along which we exist, which we rend or enhance. Living nature is to be avenged for crimes committed against it.

Most important, murder is not forever to be legal. In Revelation, it bears repeating that God enters the scene as one who unmasks and hastens moral process. "Quickly" is a great word with Him: "come quickly,"... "I am coming quickly... (Rev. 12:12,20)

Moral and physical process interact, inevitably. So the earth recoils from crime, as people wreak their fury and hatred on the earth and living things. Every war is a war on ecology as well as on community; after a given time, the ground no longer supports our criminal weight.

The ultimate consumers (warmakers) eat people. That is why a loathsome banquet seems a weirdly fitting image for the end of things, the end of those who consumed the people and the earth. No God eats them.

This image bears comparison also with the "hell fires," or the Sartrian metaphor of hell as boredom, or the circles upon circles of Dante or Solzhenitsyn. Since hell is a state of spirit, we can grasp it only by imagining it. Here the violent, the deceitful, the envious, the truly sinful, prepare the banquet themselves, cook it, choose the guests. But it is all ultimately self-consuming. They do not know it, but they themselves are the menu. The goal of "life" is — extinction. Ultimately, self-extinction.

After the banquet, what? The void. Americans held such a feast, time and again during the Vietnam war; a daily body count, a menu which may have as well been venison or wild birds. People literally cannibalized others. But at the end of the ear the tables were turned, so to speak. A prelude, a revelation.

War is a kind of cannibalism. The "last day" scene is not only a banquet hall; it is a battlefield. The scene is a stereotype of history; the birds of the air come to eat the flesh of men and horses, after the battle. An obscene clean-up occurs. Those announced as the "menu" are clearly enumerated, as is often the way in Revelation. "All, both free and slave, small and great." (Rev. 19:18) No matter what their estate in the world, all are doomed, are equally grist for the grinder. The sole exception are those who have not worshipped the beast, or worshipped its image, or borne its mark. This exceptional vocation, to life rather than death, has been insisted on before. So has its price; but the price is not this noisome scene of horror.

The act of eating is an image dear to John. He had been told by the angel to "eat the little scroll"; it would be "bitter in his guts and sweet on his tongue." (Rev. 10:8) For some, Christianity is a tasters' choice; for others, a bitter pill. But "eating" is knowledge, assimilating the truth. ("I am the bread of life. He who comes to me will never be hungry; he who believes in me will never thirst." Jn. 6:35) Just as in Genesis; only there it was false knowledge. But now on the battlefield, the scene is excoriating, random, meaningless, an orgy of the carnivorous birds of the air. Because the truth was never in this air. Now the truth is pure weapon, the blade is keen; they are slain by the "sword" (word) that issues from his mouth." (Jn. 18:37) They have sinned against all four elements; now fire and water conspire to destroy them; they are thrown into "a lake of fire."

The military character of the metaphor is nonetheless perplexing. How can the God of peace announce the end of history as a "battle," with all the accoutrements, horrid sounds, smells, sights, the voracious face of wars, a banquet and battlefield? Such images, of course, do not arise in a void. They come from the unconscious and conscious activity of men and women, the history of crime, out of chaos, the sea, land, whence the beasts arise, and along with them, ourselves. The images of Revelation are about us; all our bloody history, with and without, against and for one another. In that history, declares this grotesque, nightmarish, painfully truthful book of Kells, God lifts the veil on who we are; our deceits and self-deception are unmasked, one after another peeled away.

Who are we? Let us imagine it, says God; You are sons and daughters of wrath. He starts from the fatalism of most people. ("There always were wars, there always will be.") He starts from our vile and degraded history, our "self-acceptance," which is the millennial acceptance of death as the first fact of life. From the military killers whose absurd ikons disgrace our parks and squares. From the military rites of passage, which seal the next generation with Caesar's baptismal mark : "Vowed to violence; kill, be killed." From our military budget, the killer toys of general and colonels. He shows us — ourselves, shows us slouching along our field of history, which is, inevitably, a battlefield. Shows us literally feeding off the dead; since in our horrid economy and ecology of death, nothing is to be wasted, save life itself. We feed off the dead of My Lai, the nuclear dead of Hiroshima, the natives of Wounded Knee, Salvadorans. Who of us has not fed off the dead?

He offers us also (dare we admit it?) the kind of God most of us want, most of the time. Not a God of history, not the God of Jesus, that unconscionable lion and lamb; not the God who preemptorily orders Peter to put up his sword; not the God of Calvary, in fine — that ultimately outrageous non-inquisitorial victim and victor. Not such a God, it goes without saying (it can hardly be said), to Christian millionaires and munitions makers and lockstep academics and mute racists and money-grubbing clerics.

He starts, this nightmarish master of psychic darkness, with the gods most of us secretly cherish and constantly worship; the gods we roll out of our bunkers and laboratories and napalm factories and anti-personnel experiments. That true god, "true blue," preeminently and idolatrously false; false as our own false faces, our devious hearts. The god of unlimited violence, of first-strike capacity, of Mutual Assured Destruction (MAD), of war games, war scenarios, the gods of our way of life (of death).

The implication of the nightmare! There is no path to true worship, to "the sight of his face" (Ps. 23), except by the exorcism of our false gods. True worship, within the church as without, waits on the end of idolatry — within the church as without.

The cynics are very nearly right; war nearly has the last word. That nearness, that pretense to the last word, the pretense that the last word is the only right word, that one only word — death — sums up all possible words, and in the process, quite snuffs out life itself as bearing the meaning of existence — that pretense is accepted everywhere. No pretense at all, but a quite legitimate and sensible claim. What else is new?

Revelation calls a halt. War is not ultimate, though it is fiercely penultimate. It has a death grip on us, body and soul. It wants us, body and soul: to know it, to love it, to serve it in this world, to be its prey forever. We must take that seriously; war seems to have the edge, up close, right up to, almost including, the end of things. It would like to seize the end as well. "One more push," exulted Churchill at the Rhine.

If this is so, if violence is so deeply a part of us almost to define our fate, if our soul is a sheathed sword, God Himself must take all this into account. Which He does. He imagines us — so to speak — truthfully; as we are, not as a moonstruck doting parent would fantasize us.

Toward the end of the banquet episode, a kind of anticlimax occurs. There seems in fact to have been no battle at all, after all the fanfare and lineup! The enemy was hell-bent, Beast and false prophet; violence and untruth joined hands. But their followers were not even granted the brave dignity of a good fight. They seem simply to have fallen over, dead on their feet. Their own idolatry, untruth and violence touched them, a finger of plague. They were meat on the hoof. Now they are eaten — which seems in any event to have been their destiny, self-chosen.

(It is also worth noting that the images of war and battle have parallel images in Revelation: judgment, crisis, blindness, darkness, second death.)

We are so impregnated with violence, this scene of battle suggests, that we do not hesitate to make our vile history into God's own, our conduct His; our images, nightmares, obsessions, enemies, His own. And finally, our debased image of God meets and melds with our debased image of ourselves. And we are appalled, as well we might be. We had dreamed of a heavenly banquet; we were granted an orgy in hell. Which of these did we really want, long for, fantasize, all along?

The terrible battle scenes of Revelation seem vivid enough to give comfort to the hawk in us, powerful and bloody enough to discourage the most peaceable. But such reactions are strictly out of context, and therefore miss the point. The key is the immanent imagination; that storehouse of the ages which Jung has explored. In scriptures, these massed data are not wiped out, as though electric shock must be applied to humanity before we could know ourselves or God. Far from it. God's word comes to confront this imagination, to purify it also; and most of all to show forth its outcome.

The battle is also within. No one of us but is deep split, like a gourd struck by an ax blade. "The good that I would do I do not do; the evil I would avoid I perform." (Rm. 7:19) Rare is the human being whose psychic life does not make him a terrifying problem to himself.

The psyche is in the world; the whole world is in the soul. We seek a resolution, but the elements of terror and death seem only to multiply, put off, derange, proliferate their madness.

History cannot answer for history; the prophets prove false, or debase themselves into a herd of pseudo-futurologists, no more worthy of respect than star gazers.

And in public life the political machinery is rigorously anti-human, militarized; the people grow desperate; they see no place for decency, compassion, vindication of the innocent. They are fed a diet of "wars and rumors of war"; and the diet turns them into ghosts.

It all seems to be coming true; scripture verifies the nightmare. This is by no means said to our comfort. When any one people all but possess the earth, everybody else on earth becomes a threat. The response, commonly known as "diplomacy," is that of a village bully: off with your coats, gloves on. Such a people, controlling, parrying, bullying, conspiring, killing, long to bring off, the sooner the better, a big showdown.

Revelation stages just such a battle; says in effect: See, this is how God sees you.

The Nightmare of God

When people bend scripture to their own uses (how often this has happened, justifying the worst crimes!), perhaps one had best take a more careful look at scripture. Today the divided soul of the human race has drawn a line, across which a battle of extinction is announced. (It seems worth noting that the doomsday aspects of the battle are entirely Western: technology, world domination, cold war, the shootout, the shutdown.)

The battle proceeds, an attempt to extinguish "the camp of saints and the beloved city." (Rev. 20:9) This is the meaning of that East-West face-off which in both places would stamp out evidence of goodness, of nonviolent resistance, of political decency within its ranks; would destroy the people of "refusal," those who go about the business of love, concern, justice, under the very heel of God and Magog. Truly they form a "camp"; they are in concentration camps, work camps, prison camps, here, there, in every place where civil power declares them non-persons, non-cogs, non-cooperators. In "camps"; their lives are precarious, edgy, ignorant of tomorrow, on the move, uncaring about securities wrung from the misery of others. And they form the "beloved city" in the image of the "beloved disciple" to whom the vision was once granted. They are building, even now, the celestial city of Jerusalem, whose cornerstone is justice, where "all tears and mourning will be wiped away." (Rev. 21:4)

Thus the battle scene *is* the judgment scene. These are mutual metaphors; the one leads to the other, mutual source of insight. In order that the super state may function smoothly, wrote Morocz, the Ukrainian resister of conscience, all citizens must become cogs. Magog and the cogs. Not to bear his imprint, which makes everyone like everyone else, souls in lockstep, the penalty as well as the reward must be clear: soul in lockup. The penalty (Rev. 13) clears the public scene of deviants, either by execution or by exclusion from the life of the community. That was the preliminary; a kind of cold war solution to the "problem" of political and religious dissidents — two areas that of course often coincide.

Now, says Revelation, the meaning of that final battle which is also a final judgment, becomes a little clearer. Both Gog and Magog move against that conscientious remnant which has proved, in fact, inextinguishable, because it coincides with human goodness itself, the life-giving and life-preserving soul of the race.

The battle has suicidal aspects: It is the self-consummation of the first, foremost, largest, best consumer society; Babylon, in fact, whose demise, one recalls, was mourned most deeply by the merchants of the earth. We do well to give the images their proper scope. The "fire from heaven" is both visitation and flareup. It is a figure of human goodness, stifled underground, seeking to vindicate itself against overwhelming odds. Gog and Magog marshaled all power against it, set as they are on self-destruction as a way of destroying all. The fire is also an image of the kindling of stubborn, slow-moving history by the Lord of history. The mills of the gods may grind slowly, but the mill of God is both speedy and fine.

Just as every world battle, and every courtroom, and every secure prison contain forces long hidden, long controlled, twitching in the hands of special interests and devious minds, of politics, dickering — so here, long, age-long, accreting, ignored, unrequited, injustice grew and grew, a cancer claiming the dying world. Now it has burst. The image is apt: a "fire from heaven" corresponding to a fire in the bowels of "the camp of the saints, the beloved city." A conflagration of love, outraged and stifled, has broken out.

The battle, as we saw in a prior scene that is certainly parallel (Rev. 19:17) is no battle at all; it is a rout. And even that word seems mild in face of the utter defeat of the powers of the earth. They are simply swept aside like petty images of clay in a child's battlefield game. They are of no account, they are quickly disposed of; on the day they had reckoned their victory, they are swept into the rubble of time, debris on debris, beyond serious regard or notice.

Thus the dignity of God, and the dignity of the wretched and defeated of the earth, the impoverished and exploited, are simultaneously put in a new light. The powers of this world, inflated beyond bearing, move to bring an end to history; just as they had presumed to set history in motion, to move it along, a mighty current, the empery of the Great Powers, their diplomacy, their city-trading, their colonies and "spheres of influence," their wars, their (truly) gross production. But in their view, even this was not enough. Power, such power, moves inevitably, inexorably, toward an Armageddon; it must have things clear, tidy, final, on its own terms.

Things indeed shall be made clear. But on utterly different terms. This is God's promise; we are to abide by it.

Afterword

by Tom Lewis-Borbely

I begin this reflection the Summer of 1999, having just returned from federal prison, LSC/Allenwood, Pennsylvania. My original Afterword for this book was written in 1981. It is important to recognize that little has changed since then for the people we call poor in the United States. The prison I come from is filled with God's poor. They come to prisons not only from the cities of the United States, but also from all over the world, namely the Third World. There is an immigration court right in the prison. One can hear every language in the world spoken, the primary being Spanish.

It is what I call the quiet time here in the city, the hours between 5:30 a.m. and 9:30 a.m. After that everything wakes up for another day of city life. I just dropped Andrea off for her commute to Boston. She is studying about producing and filming documentaries. Then, quality care for our eight-year-old daughter Nora. I made this commitment coming from jail knowing that my personal artwork, from prison sketches and new ideas, will be put on hold, so to say. I am doing some artwork with Nora and her friends, allowing for new work to emerge from this experience.

Tomorrow I will return to pray with the Trappist monks at St. Joseph Abbey. I have been doing this early morning prayer and Mass once a week since the mid 80s. The monks' donation of food and Trappist jelly has always been a blessing for Catholic Worker friends. The Mustard Seed Catholic Worker soup kitchen still serves the daily meal to neighbors and others. I wrote my original Afterword from the Mustard Seed 18 years ago.

Now we live across the street from the Mustard Seed and call our nonviolent community Emma House, named after Emma Young, an African American who lived with us for many years before she died in the early 90s. Mari, Andrea's mother who lives with us, will continue to fill the surrounding corners with her beautiful flowers, personally recognized last week at a neighborhood festival.

We are scheduling another "street Mass" in August. These Catholic Masses began in 1992, the first celebrant, Fr. Steve Kelly, S.J., an "image of hope" in the streets. August 6th and 9th will be remembered with friends in an anti-nuclear protest.

So much left unsaid as I prepare to rise early with a request from Nora to pray with me at the Abbey.

Returning to a portion of the original Afterword:

" 'I have always believed that an artist is an artist, in jail or out of jail. So there I was in my studio, a four by six cell. My art materials were limited ... I managed to get a few sheets of sketch paper, a small bottle of India ink; but there was not enough black for the poems, so I added a mixture of ground cigarette ashes and water. For the brown background I mixed a combination of instant coffee and cocoa. Finally I shaped a few popsicle sticks into pens....'

"Those remarks are from my introduction to Daniel Berrigan's book, *Trial Poems*, on which we collaborated in jail shortly after the Catonsville Nine draft board raid near Baltimore during Vietnam. Now, approximately ten years later, Dan and I have collaborated on yet another book with roots that are anchored in the prison experience.

"But the art work this time is technically better, photo etchings, originally 18" x 24" in reduced form especially for this book. And the text this time is much more elaborate and developed.

"Yet in spite of the time span, technical improvements, and personal artistic changes, there remains one constant, one connecting, indeed, one sustaining element: prison. Since Catonsville, its consequences, and through the 1970s, prison has been the primary thread by which Dan and I and our friends have stayed together.

"The subjects of these etchings are our friends, our lives. I took the photos as I participated with friends in demonstrations, acts of war resistance, celebrations, jail over the last decade. The art is about friends and for friends who repeatedly risk prison because not to in these nuclear-mad times is to die.

"I do not mean to be flip about jail. I speak of the experience in a humble way. From my most recent short incarceration to the three years I did for Catonsville, prison has helped me grow. Prison, especially in a Nuclear Age, provides one with a good opportunity to make a personal retreat, to reflect on or take stock of one's life, to meditate, and yes, to pray.

"For as many times as I have gone there, jail is always difficult. It never gets any easier. When preparing for acts of civil disobedience I am always full of anxiety, particularly about prison.

"But the prison experience never seems to dull the edge of our lives. Rather, it keeps that edge sharp, our minds sane, and our direction clear. It is the Nuclear Age that is calculated to dull our senses with false security and an illusion of hope, a hope which in fact is death.

> *The second wild beast was then permitted to give life to the beast's image, so that the image had the power of speech and of putting to death anyone who refused to worship it. It forced all people, small and great, rich and poor, slave and free, to accept a stamped image on their right hand or their forehead....* (Rev. 14:15-17)

"Dan and I and our friends believe that to stay alive through the 1980s one

The Nightmare of God

must risk or enter jail for nonviolent resistance to the Nuclear Beast. Otherwise we are dead even before the very first strike is made. This is the burden anyone who wishes to remain alive in this Nuclear Age must carry.

"This book truly comes out of prison. John, the author of The Book of Revelation which Dan has so eloquently interpreted in these pages, was a prisoner on the tiny island of Patino (Patmos). He was sent there for witnessing to the words and works of Jesus. (Rev. 1:9-10) Dan begins this book in prison. My sketches were done in prison where I did time for protesting nuclear weapons. Much of the editing by Sunburst publisher Johnny Baranski was done in prison where he spent six months for resisting the Trident nuclear weapon system. Some of the editing was done by Margie Farren, a Catholic Worker whose tasks were interrupted by jail time for protesting the MX-C3 missile system.

"Prison is what this book is all about, not only for poets and artists who want to continue with a vision of hope in these seemingly hopeless times, but for everyone. This book, from prison, invites you to resist the Nuclear Madness."

I end this reflection with a harsh question to myself as well as to friends. The United States will continue to build new prisons; it is the largest growth industry in America. Philosophies of various prison reform will come and go, but prison will remain as well as the poor in prisons.

Are we who have been practicing the Works of Mercy also called to the blessing of praying with the poor in prison not as a visitor, but as a prisoner?

www.ingramcontent.com/pod-product-compliance
Lightning Source LLC
Chambersburg PA
CBHW070924160426
43193CB00011B/1570